# REAL FRAUDS FOUND IN NFPs

**BY LYNDA DENNIS, PH.D., CPA, CGFO**

## Notice to readers

*Real Frauds Found in NFPs* is intended solely for use in continuing professional education and not as a reference. It does not represent an official position of the American Institute of Certified Public Accountants, and it is distributed with the understanding that the author and publisher are not rendering legal, accounting, or other professional services in the publication. This course is intended to be an overview of the topics discussed within, and the author has made every attempt to verify the completeness and accuracy of the information herein. However, neither the author nor publisher can guarantee the applicability of the information found herein. If legal advice or other expert assistance is required, the services of a competent professional should be sought.

**You can qualify to earn free CPE through our pilot testing program.
If interested, please visit https://aicpacompliance.polldaddy.com/s/pilot-testing-survey.**

ISBN 978-1-119-72326-4 (paper)
ISBN 978-1-119-72325-7 (ePDF)
ISBN 978-1-119-72328-8 (ePub)
ISBN 978-1-119-72327-1 (obk)

Course Code: **746572**
CL4RFNF GS-0419-0B
Revised: **February 2020**

V10018882_061020

# Table of Contents

Chapter 1

# Case 1: Misappropriation of Benefits

## Learning objectives

- Determine how benefits might be misappropriated in a fictitious not-for-profit (NFP) entity.

- Use the fraud triangle in light of operations at offsite locations in a fictitious NFP.

## Before we start

Fraud risks associated with benefit programs can sometimes be overlooked because there is typically no physical asset relating to the benefit. Program benefits provided by NFPs may be provided to beneficiaries that do not qualify for the benefit or do not qualify for the level of benefit provided include the following:

- Unemployment
- Food stamps
- Housing assistance
- Financial aid
- Healthcare
- Legal assistance
- Child care
- Membership
- Education

Indicators that program benefits might be misappropriated include the following:

- Copies of missing application forms and underlying supporting documentation
- Participant files lacking required information (for example, interview sheets, tax returns, and so on)
- Decentralized intake centers or centralized intake centers with little or no monitoring by management or supervisory personnel
- Inadequately trained or supervised program personnel
- Inadequate or ineffective controls over program assets
- Lack of periodic physical inventories of program assets

## Background

Level Field Preschool is a large regional NFP organized under IRC Section 501 (c)(3), controlling and operating five preschool education and child care facilities in three counties. The population served by Level Field is primarily low-income families residing in the county where the education/child care facility is located. The primary sources of revenue for Level Field are various education and child care state grants (80%). These revenues are augmented with fees for program services (5%) and contributions from the United Way and the community (15%). Fees for program services are assessed on a sliding scale using family size and household income to determine the fee amount.

Each location is operated by a director and is staffed with teachers, student aides, and childcare assistants based on the number of students enrolled in the preschool education and child care programs. In addition, each location has a bookkeeper who is responsible for processing daily cash receipts and preparing the deposit. The location director takes the locked bank bag to the bank for deposit whenever there are receipts for deposit and the bookkeeper notifies the administrative office of the deposit amount and date. All receiving reports and invoices for goods/services received/provided at the locations are approved by the director and sent to the administrative office for payment.

Operational oversight responsibility is performed by administrative office staff who are based in the downtown education/child care facility. Each location director hires and fires all personnel needed to operate the location. However, all job postings, recruiting, and background checks are done by the human resources department at the administrative office. Employees track their time on a daily basis using a cloud-based time management system. Supervisors electronically approve the time submitted and release the information for processing by administrative office staff. Due to the nature of the child care industry, and high turnover rates of Level Field teachers, aides, and assistants, payroll is processed on a weekly basis.

Level Field refers to its five locations as the Downtown location, East Side location, West Side location, South Side location, and the North Side Location. State grants relating to the various preschool education programs are awarded for five years and are awarded at the location level rather than at the entity-wide level. The state requires Level Field to undergo a financial statement and compliance audit each year. State grants for child care programs are awarded for three years, subject to annual availability, at an entity-wide level. The chief executive officer (CEO), vice president of operations (VPO), and chief financial officer (CFO) allocate the child care grant funds to the five locations based on a child-driven formula. Grant compliance for all grants is delegated to each location director.

## Knowledge check

1. Which is accurate of Level Field?

   a. Level Field receives 10% of revenues from fees for program services.
   b. Level Field is a United Way agency.
   c. Level Field operates in a five-county area.
   d. Level Field is heavily dependent on community contributions to fund its programs.

2. Which is accurate of Level Field?

   a. Location directors post job vacancies, recruit, and perform background checks for location employees.
   b. Level Field uses manual time sheets for employees to log hours worked.
   c. Operational oversight responsibility is performed by administrative office staff who are housed in the downtown education/child care facility.
   d. Payroll is processed on a biweekly basis.

## The case

*The following discussion takes place after-hours at the unofficial teacher happy hour staff meeting between Downtown teachers Kelly Carter, Amanda Miller, and Brittany Nelson.*

"Hey Amanda, you know what really bothers me about Level Field?"

"No Brittany, I don't know what really bothers you. Why don't you tell me?"

"Wait, Amanda. I know what Brittany is going to say because it is what bothers me the most as well."

"Well, go ahead, Kelly. I may only be two weeks on the job but I'm all ears."

"All right. You know how we can have a certain number of families in the program who don't meet the low-income threshold?"

"Uh, hello, Kelly. I've only been here two weeks and have no clue what you mean."

"Kels, give it up. Let me explain it as I am the one who asked the question in the first place."

"All right, Brittany you do it. Age before beauty after all."

"As I was trying to say a few minutes ago, the thing bothering me the most is we seem to be accepting all of these families into the program with higher incomes and putting the low-income families on the waiting list. I assume we aren't exceeding the maximum allowed in the program but it doesn't seem right to be letting the higher income families take away a spot from the low-income families."

"Amanda, are you sure this is going on because it doesn't sound right. I don't think we had anything else like this at my last job. You know the main reason I left my old job for this one was because Level Field focuses on providing preschool education and child care services to only low-income families. At least this is what I was told by HR when I interviewed."

"That's what Brittany and I were told when we interviewed as well. We had our brand new early childhood education degrees looking to make the world a better place working in an inner-city preschool. Boy, did we drink the Kool-Aid."

"We all may have drunk the Kool-Aid but maybe we can do something to change things."

"What do you mean, Amanda? We are only barely experienced preschool teachers. What could we really do?"

"I'm not sure yet, Kelly, but give me some time to check on a few things, then I'll get back with you and Brittany about what I learn."

"Sounds good. Let's do this again next Friday and see what you find out, Amanda."

*The following discussion takes place between East Side Director Dana Curran, North Side Director Karen Durham, and Downtown Director Rich Hawkins, before the monthly directors' meeting held at the administrative offices. South Side Director Pat Simmons joins them later.*

"Hi there, Karen. How are things going out in the northern tundra?"

"That's not really funny, Rich. This cold weather makes it hard for our students to stay warm at home. The cold is also keeping parents from bringing their kids in for school. We are always under pressure to meet state performance measures, and kids not coming to class doesn't help us meet those goals."

"I hear you, Karen. At least you don't have the CEO and VPO breathing down your neck and popping into classes all the time. At least once a week someone at the top reminds me how important it is to keep our quality high and the enrollment at capacity. It is getting harder and harder to keep our program quality high with the cuts the Legislature keeps making in grant funding. I get we need to keep the state happy to keep the grant money coming in but sometimes the pressure is too much."

"Hey guys. Have we started yet?"

"Hi Dana and, no, we haven't started. I was blowing off steam about how much pressure we are all under to keep enrollments at capacity and how hard it is to provide higher quality with less funding."

"Yes, Karen and I are really lucky being offsite. I know we only see the VPO at East Side when he thinks we have a problem. What about you, Karen?"

"About the same, Dana. Thankfully, North Side is quite a hike from Downtown, which means we don't see a lot of the VPO. I don't really mind it when he does come up but I wish he really understood how hard we work to keep things running smoothly."

"I couldn't help but overhear you and Karen talking and I agree with everything you said. On a happier note, I may have something to help our families struggling to keep warm this winter. Pat out at South Side told me about a new state program last week. She said it provides a flat subsidy amount to help low-income families with heating bills and it is fairly easy to complete the application paperwork. Where is she, by the way? Oh, here she comes. Hi, Pat."

"Hey guys. Did I miss anything important?"

"Only the usual complaining about having to achieve higher program quality with less money. We were also discussing how the cold weather is affecting our attendance numbers and our families. Dana was about to tell us about the assistance program you discussed with her last week."

"You're right, Rich, Dana and I did talk about this last week. The program may seem a little too good to be true because it is easy to apply for and be approved. The maximum subsidy is $600 and it's based on income and family size like our program requirements. It is only a one-time amount though, which may not go very far if this cold weather continues much longer."

"It sounds like something our East Side families could qualify for and it is certainly something to help them with their utility bills. Maybe our new CFO, Amy Wallace, knows more about this. I have to get back to the center as soon as our meeting ends, but Rich you're right here. Do you have some time after the meeting to stop by her office?"

"Sure, Dana, I can drop by and ask her about this program."

*The following discussion takes place the following week at another after-hours unofficial teacher happy hour between Downtown teachers Kelly Carter, Amanda Miller, and Brittany Nelson. They are joined by two South Side teachers, Ryan Cavanaugh and Jeremy Gregg.*

"Hi guys. I hope you don't mind but I brought two friends of mine who teach at the South Side location. Meet Ryan and Jeremy. Ryan, Jeremy, meet Kelly and Amanda."

"No problem, Brittany. The more the merrier. Someone snag our server and let's order. In the meantime, what did you learn this week, Amanda? Did you have time to find out anything about the mix of low-income and non-low-income families?"

"Hold on, Kelly. Let me give the server my drink order first."

"Come on, Amanda. Where are your priorities? Just kidding."

"What are you guys talking about? Anyone feel like cluing me and Jeremy in to the conversation?"

*Kelly and Brittany explain what they discussed the previous week and how Amanda was going to research the issue and report back tonight.*

"All right. I think Jeremy and I have it now. You may not believe this but I have heard of this before. My cousin works at one of the Big 4 accounting firms . . ."

"The 'Big 4', Ryan? Is this like a college basketball playoff bracket?"

"No, Kelly, it's not. I'm not really sure what accounting firms do but apparently the 'Big 4' do a lot of different things and serve a lot of different types of clients. Yes, there are only four *really big* firms, hence 'Big 4'. My cousin works at one of them in DC and has worked on a lot of not-for-profit clients over the last two years. He was telling me at Thanksgiving how surprised I would be at the number of people who receive federal benefits without meeting the program qualifications."

"You mean like doctors doing all kinds of procedures and tests because Medicare pays for it? This is my grandad's No. 1 complaint about healthcare for seniors."

"Not quite Jeremy. My cousin told me about some programs for which people provide false documentation to prove how much they make in order to receive a bigger benefit. He also told me about some public housing program for which people were paying staff to put their name at the top of the waiting list. According to him, you can find all kinds of government reports on the internet reporting this stuff."

"I hate to interrupt you Ryan, but I'd really like to talk about what I learned this week about our program. Oh look, our drinks are here."

"No problem, Amanda. Here's your wine, Kelly, and here's your beer, Brittany. Amanda, are you good with your Cosmo?"

"Yes, and no more interruptions. I don't have a cousin at a Big 4 firm but I do have a roommate who works at one here in town. She helped me look up information on the state website about the requirements of our preschool education program. I understand totally what learning objectives our programs are supposed to achieve and the programs we use to do this. But, the stuff my roommate found sounded like a foreign language to me. She did give me some information in plain English though."

"Spit it out, Amanda."

"Patience, Brittany. According to what she found, we can have up to 10% of the families in our program with income above 120% of the state poverty level. I think she said these families are called 'over income' families or something like that. Families with incomes below the 120% are 'under income' families. Also, there are limits to the maximum number of kids any one location can have."

"Wow, I never was good at math but even I can see where this is going."

"You're right, Jeremy. With a limited enrollment, over income families take away spots under income families would otherwise fill which is what Kelly, Brittany, and I discussed here last week. Ryan, based on what your cousin said do you think 'over income' people might be paying staff at the Downtown location to be put on their waiting list? Our program has some of the best success stories and has been recognized as a Preschool of Excellence the last 10 years."

"I don't know, Amanda, but it is something to think about. Our program at South Side is not as prestigious as yours, and our demographics are very different, but we do pretty well at holding our own. We have a number of families a little better off than others who pay part of the tuition. Do you think anyone might have used fake income information to avoid having to pay tuition?"

"Anything is possible, Ryan. Oh look, here's our food. Let's eat."

"Good idea, Kelly. Why don't we all see if we can find out if anything like this is going on in our programs and then report back next Friday?"

*Over the next week, Kelly, Brittany, and Amanda start paying more attention to conversations of staff and parents and becoming more aware of the atmosphere outside of the classroom. One day in the breakroom, Amanda hears the following conversation between teacher's aide, Susan Andrews, and the bookkeeper, Janice Weatherly.*

"Don't you shush me, I'm telling you, Susan, something is going on here."

"Janice, I've told you to quit watching all those true crime shows. You are starting to see things where they don't exist."

"Really, dreaming things, Susan? What do you think about the two new families we let in after the holiday break?"

"We had two spots open up before Thanksgiving and we filled them is what I think."

"What if I told you the surnames of those two families happen to be the maiden name of our esteemed director's wife and his daughter-in-law? What does this tell you?"

"Well, I don't know. How do you know this anyway, Janice?"

"You know I've always wanted to be Columbo; it's in my DNA. It makes me suspicious of all kinds of things. When I saw the cars the two moms drove up in, my Spidey sense started tingling. I'm not one to judge but if you can afford a relatively new luxury SUV I don't think you qualify for our subsidized preschool program."

"Janice, you know how judging gets you in trouble. Driving a nice new car could mean someone took advantage of one of those car loan programs they are always advertising during the 11pm news."

"Well, in this case, Susan, you would be wrong. I looked up the surnames using the state databases. From there, it was easy to trace them back to Rich and his daughter-in-law. I looked them up on social media, too. You wouldn't believe the seven-day cruise one of them went on over the holidays."

"Janice, it still doesn't mean they didn't qualify for our program."

"You can be as naïve as you want to be, Susan. I know what I know and those two families do not qualify for our low-income program. They are taking a spot away from one of our truly deserving families."

"They may have been let in for a good reason, you know. Besides, maybe they are paying customers."

"Susan, in the 25 years I have been here we have never had anyone in our program with enough money to have a new luxury SUV. If our community found out we are accepting families who don't qualify when we have a waiting list of 200 families, they would be outraged. As for paying tuition, I am the bookkeeper. Don't you think I would know if they were paying tuition?"

"Well, I guess you would know who pays and who doesn't. What are we going to do?"

*Amanda leaves the breakroom a few minutes after Janice and Susan leave and texts Brittany, Kelly, Ryan, and Jeremy "Can't wait to spill 411. C u @ stf mtg Fri. ☺"*

*Two weeks after the directors' meeting, Dana Curran calls Rich Hawkins to follow up with him about the low-income subsidy program they discussed before the meeting.*

"Hi, Rich. This is Dana. Is this a good time? I purposely called during student nap time to try and catch you."

"Good call on your part, Dana, as I have a bit of time right now. What can I do for you?"

"I wondered if you had a chance to find out any more information about the subsidy to help low-income families with their power bills. This cold front seems to have taken up residence over the region and they aren't forecasting warmer temps any time soon. Our families could really use some help."

"I meant to follow up with you and Karen but things have been crazy with open enrollment going on the past two weeks. It seems our program here becomes more popular every year and a lot of people want their kids in it. Right now I'm looking at a waiting list of three years based on our current enrollment capacity."

"No problem, I certainly understand. We have a different income demographic out here at East Side but we still have more families needing our program than we have openings. Was Amy able to give you any information?"

"She gave me a lot of good information and links to the program's website. The subsidy is for a flat amount, which is $300 for a single individual and $600 for a family of any size. It is based on income and uses the same 120% of the state poverty level we use to qualify our preschool families. You can apply for the subsidy online via their website or go to one of the state Health and Human Services offices. If you want, I'll send you the link to their website."

"Thanks, Rich. I'll get it posted for our families and on our website as soon as I get it from you."

"No problem, Dana. See you in two weeks."

*Later the same day, Dana calls Pat Simmons, South Side director, to thank her for mentioning the program.*

"Hey Pat. This is Dana at East Side. Do you have a minute?"

"Sure. My teachers have everything under control right now, which means I have time to breathe. What can I do for you?"

"I wanted to thank you for mentioning the power subsidy program the state has. Rich talked to Amy about it and he gave me the information today. This will be extremely helpful for our families here at East Side."

"You're welcome but I didn't really do much. I let our families here at South Side know about it last month. Several families applied a few weeks ago and received their checks this past week. I guess this extended cold weather has motivated the state to get these benefits disbursed sooner rather than later."

"Well, I think it's a win-win. Thanks again for the info. See you at the next directors' meeting."

*The next day at the South Side location, Ryan arrives earlier than usual and walks to Pat's office to let her know he is going to start the coffee. Before he reaches Pat's office, he hears her talking on the phone and turns to go to the breakroom but stops when he hears Pat mention a low-income program she is scamming.*

"I'm telling you, Karen, this is the easiest scam I've ever run. I started by simply using names and addresses I found on social media sites and the Internet White Pages. Last week, I came up with the idea to apply 'on behalf' of our families..."

"Yes, that's what I'm trying to tell you. The state folks processing these applications are trying to get the checks out as quickly as possible in order to help people keep their power on during this cold weather. They don't seem to be comparing any information to any database and all you have to provide is proof of income."

"What do you mean it's hard to get people to hand over proof of income? I used my weekly pay stub and told them it was a monthly pay stub. I know what income level they use because it's the same one we use here."

"You don't have to use a pay stub. They take a letter from an employer or a tax return as proof of income. Rich told me how to dummy up a letter and how to use the 1040 tax form at www.irs.gov. All you have to do is bring up the form and input bogus information. It doesn't save to the IRS database so you only need to print it and use it as proof of income."

"Oh yeah, what I was saying about our families. I learned about this program several months ago from a friend of mine who works at HHS. We weren't having weather issues then and I didn't remember it until this cold front moved in last month. Don't judge me, but I really didn't mention it to our families. Listening to the parents talk when they picked up their kids, I figured none of them knew about the program. I used their names and income information and applied 'on their behalf' for the benefit. You have access to all the family information in your files there at North Side, don't you?"

"You are two steps ahead of me. I set up a post office box at a place in an almost abandoned strip mall a few weeks ago to use as the mailing address. By the time the state figures it out, I'll have closed it down and no one will be the wiser, well, except for you. In the meantime, if you want to use it let me know and I'll give you the details."

"Oops, I hear someone in the breakroom. Gotta go. Talk to you later."

## Knowledge check

3. Which is accurate of Level Field?

    a. Amanda Miller, Kelly Carter, and Brittany Nelson are teachers at the Downtown location.
    b. Pat Simmons is the director for the Downtown location.
    c. Rich Hawkins is the director for the South Side location.
    d. Jeremy Gregg has a cousin who works for a Big 4 firm in DC.

## Exercises

1. What elements of the fraud triangle[1] (that is, opportunity, incentive or pressure, and rationalization or attitude), if any, are present in this case?

2. What procedures could have been in place to ensure eligibility and waiting list requirements were met?

3. What, if any, internal controls are missing or inadequate, which might indicate there is a potential for fraud in this case?

4. What types of preliminary audit procedures might detect this situation? What types of other audit procedures might detect this situation?

---

[1] Paragraph .11 of AU-C section 240, *Consideration of Fraud in a Financial Statement Audit* (AICPA *Professional Standards)* (see course appendix A) states three conditions are generally present when fraud occurs: opportunity, incentive or pressure, and rationalization or attitude. These three conditions are commonly referred to as the fraud triangle. Paragraph 11(b) of ISA section 240, *The Auditor's Responsibility Relating to Fraud in an Audit of Financial Statements*, does not include rationalization or attitude as a fraud risk factor.

Chapter 2

# Case 2: Grant Expense Allocations

## Learning objective

- Analyze how procurement and expense allocation policies in a fictitious not-for-profit (NFP) entity can be circumvented and lead to possible fraud.

## Before we start

Grantors and grant recipients may have a long-term and close relationship that could create fraud risks. For example, an NFP may be the only organization in a rural area that is able to provide certain services to a targeted population. Likewise, an NFP may have an excellent reputation in the community or region relating to the provision of specific types of services. In these situations, a grantor might be willing to provide less oversight to such organizations in exchange for the NFP providing exclusive or high-quality services (or both) to program beneficiaries.

Allocation of grant expenses can be a complex area if an entity has a number of grants from various grantors, with different compliance requirements, or complex compliance requirements.

An inherent fraud risk in NFPs receiving grants is they may feel pressure to misstate functional amounts to comply with grant provisions or debt covenants. Additionally, mission-driven employees and directors may be willing to allocate unallowable costs to grants in order to provide more program services.

# Background

Happy Campers, Inc. is a 501(c)(3) corporation whose mission is to enrich the lives of at-risk elementary and middle-school aged children through a quality summer camp experience. The organization has been in existence for 30 years and is widely recognized for the success and diversity of its camping programs. Funding sources for Happy Campers include federal grants (50%), state grants (25%), contributions (15%), United Way (5%), and charges for services (5%).

Elementary age campers attend a day camp and middle school age campers attend an overnight camp. All camp sessions are for one week and held Monday through Friday from 8am to 6pm for elementary campers and Sunday afternoon to Friday afternoon for middle-school age campers. Day camp sessions are held at the Happy Campers facility and overnight camp sessions are held at a privately-owned campground.

In addition to recreational and social activities, campers also participate in various educational programs relating to drug education, avoiding gangs, study habits, self-esteem, and other character-building sessions. Several individual federal and state grants fund the specific educational programs whereas a large federal grant covers the operating costs of the day and overnight camps.

Happy Campers constructed its facility several years ago using contributions from the community and various foundation, federal, and state grants. A wealthy and reclusive philanthropist owns the campground, which he leases to Happy Campers for $1,000 per month. As part of the agreement, Happy Campers provides all maintenance of the campground on a year-round basis.

During the school year when students have a scheduled day off, Happy Campers offers half-day educational programs at its facility, which are provided at no cost to parents. After-session child care is offered for working parents with fees charged on a sliding scale based on household income and family size. These sessions are funded with contributions because no grant funding is available.

Because Happy Campers operates primarily from mid-May to mid-August, it has few full-time employees. All camp staff, except for the camp director and maintenance coordinator, are part-time seasonal employees. Full-time personnel include the executive director, camp director, maintenance coordinator, and administrative assistant. The executive director and camp director have been with Happy Campers for 10 years and all have extensive experience in working with at-risk youth. The maintenance coordinator was hired three years ago and has been through two summer camp sessions. The administrative assistant has been with the organization for more than 25 years.

The executive director's responsibilities include overseeing day-to-day operations, fundraising, and grant writing. Payroll and accounting functions are included in the responsibilities of the administrative assistant whereas the camp director is in charge of all programming. In addition, the camp director supervises the maintenance coordinator. From an operational perspective, Happy Campers tracks costs for two programs, summer camps and school year sessions, and allocates costs to two support functions, management and general and fundraising.

# Knowledge check

1.  Which is accurate of Happy Campers?

    a.  Happy Campers has been in existence 30 years.
    b.  The only program is an overnight camp program for middle-school age children.
    c.  There are no programs held during the school year.
    d.  Most of the funding for Happy Campers is from contributions.

# The case

*The following conversation occurs between executive director, Grace Patel, camp director, Ric Alvarez, and the assistant director of the state Health and Human Services Department (HHS) at the annual United Way kickoff luncheon.*

"I don't know why you have to drag me to this event every year, Grace. We don't get a lot of money from the United Way and every year they pass on funding our request for a new year-round mentoring program. Without their seed money, we won't ever be able to get the program up and running."

"Hush, Ric. I know how important the mentoring program is to you and we *will* get it going at some point. Look, there's Doug Frye. Let's go pick his brain about what's going on with the legislature and the budget for next year."

"Hi there, Grace, Ric. What's going on these days with your happy campers?"

"Right now, we're wrapping up what looks to be one of our most successful summers ever. We were at max capacity for all sessions in both the day and overnight camps. If we could get another campsite we could serve twice as many kids."

"Good to hear you had such a successful summer, Ric. The boss and I are hoping the legislature doesn't cut the department's budget for next year because it would be tough to have to cut programs, funding levels, or both."

"I realize the governor promised more prisons and more jobs during his campaign but surely he won't cut funding for programs designed to keep kids out of prison!"

"I wish I could say he won't, Grace, but if I were you, I'd have a 'Plan B' in place. You probably won't have to worry about funding cuts to your drug and gang education programs as they're under Department of Justice (DOJ). If they cut education funding, though, you may be looking at little or no funding for your study habits program. Hey, don't shoot me. I'm only the messenger"

"Keep us posted if you can, Doug."

"Sure thing. See you around, guys."

*A month later the legislature passes a final budget that includes significant cuts to HHS programs but increases in funding to address the state's "opioid epidemic" and fighting gang violence. Grace, Ric, and administrative assistant, Nadine Henderson are discussing what impact the budget might have on their programs in the upcoming year.*

"All right, Grace, what's our Plan B? By the way, have you heard anything from Doug lately?"

"No Ric, I haven't heard from him, but I thought I might reach out early next week after he's had a few days to deal with the fallout from the budget bombshell. For the time being, let's assume the worst and see what we can do to minimize the damage."

"Grace, what are you thinking is 'the worst'?"

"I'm not sure, Nadine, but I think we need to run multiple scenarios. We definitely need a doomsday scenario, which assumes all of our state HHS funding is cut, then maybe variations for 10, 25, and 50 percent cuts. At least we don't have to worry about cuts to the federal funds for our camp program, well at least not this year. I reached out to my contact at DOJ this morning and she doesn't feel we have anything to worry about with funding for our drug and gang programs. I haven't heard back from my contact at the Department of Education (DOE), however."

"At least this is good news, right, Grace?"

"Yes, Nadine, it is. For the scenarios, let's assume the current-year funding levels for our drug and gang programs remain the same for next year. As soon as I hear from DOE, I'll let you know what to assume for our study programs."

"Sounds good, Grace."

"All right, Grace. What's the plan for telling our parents that we don't have enough funding for their kids to come back to camp next summer?"

"Honestly, Ric, I haven't thought this far down the road. I really feel we need to see what the initial numbers show before we throw in the towel or tell parents anything. We still have several months before it's time to send out registration information."

"You know, guys, we can always try a fundraising campaign. Grace, I know we haven't done much fundraising since you took over as the director, but we used to emphasize it and we were fairly successful. You, Ric, are one of our best success stories and I think you could convince a lot of folks to open up their checkbooks."

"I don't know, Nadine. My time is already taken up doing all sorts of things for our programs but as a 'Plan C,' it's not a bad idea. In the meantime, let's run those numbers."

*Over the next few weeks, Grace, Ric, and Nadine develop a number of funding scenarios and discuss conducting a fundraising campaign. A month after the legislative budget is released, Doug Frye calls Grace with an update.*

"Hi Grace. It's Doug Frye at HHS. Do you have a few minutes to discuss your grants with us?"

"For you, Doug, I always have time. I'm already sitting down and have two cups of coffee in me so go ahead and give me the bad news."

"I hate to have to tell you this, Grace, but we are going to have to eliminate all our grants that fund administrative and general operating costs . . . "

"Wait a minute, Doug. Do you mean we won't get anything from you to cover our administrative costs? We charge very little of my time to our summer camp program and none of Nadine's, which means your grant is the only funding we have to cover these costs. Also, it's this grant that allows me to keep Ric as a full-time employee. This is not simply bad news—it's catastrophic. None of the scenarios we ran considered the apocalypse."

"Hang on a minute, Grace. I know this is bad for you but it's also bad for a lot of agencies in this state. There are a lot of folks who may have to close their doors because of this, which will leave thousands of residents without critical services and benefits."

"Sorry, Doug. Sometimes I forget the world is not all about me and Happy Campers. Is there anything good you can tell me?"

"It's not all bad news, Grace. We will be eliminating numerous positions in all of our offices throughout the state and in the capital. Doing this frees up enough money to cover a lot of what we lost in the budget process. This means we will be able to continue funding all of our current socioeconomic-based programs, such as your summer camp, but at a reduced level."

"How much of a reduction are we talking about, Doug?"

"Right or wrong, we concluded the easiest way to sell this was to reduce everyone's funding the same percentage, which works out to be 15 percent."

"Ouch, that's a pretty big hit especially on top of losing the admin funding."

"I know but it's the best we can do with what the legislature gave us. If you haven't already heard from DOJ, it should be good news when you do. They and the corrections department are the big budget winners this year."

"At least I have something positive going for me today."

"Thanks for understanding, Grace, and for not shooting the messenger. We expect to get the new grant agreements out in the next month. By the way, please don't tell anyone about the workforce reduction. We don't want a mass exodus before we have a chance to figure out how we'll operate without 10 percent of our staff."

"No problem, Doug. Talk to you later."

## Knowledge check

2. Which is **not** accurate of Happy Campers?

    a. HHS will not be able to fund any grants for administrative and general operating costs in the next year.
    b. Grants for all HHS socioeconomic programs will be reduced 15% in the next year.
    c. DOJ and the corrections department are the big budget winners in the next year.
    d. HHS does not plan to reduce staff in the next year at any of its offices.

*After talking to Doug, Grace reaches out to her contact at DOJ and learns funding for the drug and gang programs will be increased 25% from the current-year levels. Most of the increase is to extend the program to the half-day programs Happy Campers offers during the school year. Later in the afternoon, Grace's contact at DOE calls.*

"Hi Grace, it's Emily Parkes at DOE returning your call. Is this a good time?"

"Yes, Emily, it is a good time and thank you for returning my call. I was wondering if you have an idea of what is going to happen with our grant funding levels next year. We are in a bit of a crisis mode over here after learning HHS is dealing with significant cuts to their budget. They provide the vast majority of our state funds and it's going to take a lot of shuffling to keep our programs running next year."

"Obviously, I know about the HHS cuts and I am very happy the legislature saw fit to still think it important to fund education in this state. We didn't receive any additional funding but at least we aren't dealing with deep budget cuts like HHS. Actually, you were on my list of people to call today even if you hadn't contacted me first."

"Great minds think alike then, huh?"

"I'm not sure about the great mind thing on my side but we are definitely thinking along the same lines. I am happy to report we will be able to continue to fund your study and stay-in-school mentoring programs next year. We aren't through finessing everything but I know you won't receive any less than last year and there is a slight change so we may be able to get you a bit of an increase."

"This is great news, Emily. As long as there are not decreases to my current-year funding levels I am a happy camper!"

*Laughing, Emily says:*

"That was bad, Grace, even for you. I'm glad I could make your day a bit better. Talk to you next month when the new grant agreements are ready."

"Thanks, Emily."

*The following discussion occurs at the staff meeting the next morning.*

"'Mornin', Grace. I assume it's a bad news meeting since you brought doughnuts."

"You know me too well, Ric. Have a seat. Nadine went to get coffee and should back in a few minutes. Oh, here she is now."

"Now the gang is all here. Let's get this meeting started.

*Grace spends the next 20 minutes going over what she has learned about the status of their state grants and the expected funding levels. Ric and Nadine sit quietly while she goes over everything.*

"Grace, this is garbage. How are we going to run a successful program in the summer if we don't work on it all year long?"

"Calm down, Ric. I know it's tough to hear we are losing funding to cover admin and general costs. Remember, we still have the federal funding and if we launch Plan C we will hopefully raise some funds from the community to help with things. Think positive—we have money to extend the drug education and gang violence programs into the school year. I thought it would make you happy."

"I'm with Grace, Ric. It isn't as bad as it could be, and we've been thinking the worst for a while now. I'm glad all the suspense is over, and we can get to work finding a solution instead of complaining."

"Well said, Nadine. I put some numbers together last night and I think if we can raise an additional $250,000 in the next few months we can keep our capacity at last year's levels. There are a few other things we will need to do as well."

"Like what, Grace?"

"Don't hate me, Ric, but you and I will need to take over maintenance during the year because we can't afford to keep Henry as a full-time employee. I realize we may lose him altogether when we have to reduce his hours, but I am hoping he'll agree to work with us during the summer."

"Are you crazy, Grace? Who will do grant writing and fundraising if you're out at the camp picking up garbage?"

"I think Ric has a valid point, Grace. Maybe we could run numbers with Henry working part time all year long? We can also think about the percentages of your time and Ric's time that we allocate to the summer program. I have never thought the two of you charged enough time to the program. I've been here more than 25 years and I live and breathe the mission of this organization. You and Ric are the children I never had, and I don't want to see you two work this hard when there are too many other good things for you to be doing."

"Nadine, I appreciate your support but I'm not comfortable charging any more of my time, or Ric's for that matter, to the programs. Our auditors are always looking at this when they do our federal and state compliance audits."

"Every year we have at least one brand new staff auditor and one intern. I will bet you a bottle of wine we could charge all sorts of costs to our summer programs and they would never realize it."

"Nadine, I think you are letting your emotions get the best of you. Why don't we adjourn and calm down and then we can get together this afternoon to go over the numbers again."

---

*Grace leaves the room and Nadine turns to Ric and says:*

"Are you going to let them do this, Ric?"

"You know she won't listen to me or you about allocation percentages and I'm not sure why."

"It has to do with the mess she inherited from our last director. We got in a lot of trouble with the feds and the state for allocating costs to grants when they were for other things. Personally, if the old goat had asked me, I could have told him how to manipulate things in a way no one would suspect or find. Not even our auditors."

"What are you talking about, Nadine?"

"I don't want to corrupt you, Ric. Are you sure you want to hear what I have to say?"

"If it means we can keep Henry and not pressure Grace to raise twice as much in three months as she did all of last year, I'm all in."

"Don't say I didn't warn you. Let's talk about how you buy supplies for camp. You charge all of the supplies to the camp program and not to the other programs we conduct during camp."

"I know it's because we don't use them in those programs. Even if we did, it sounds like a pain to have to calculate how many pennies to charge to the drug and gang programs. I've got a camp to run and don't have time for bean counter things."

"It may sound difficult, but it really isn't. Are you willing to let me take care of things next year?"

"Sure, Nadine. Have at it."

*During the next grant-funding cycle, Nadine allocates camp supplies to all of the camp-related programs, including the specifically funded grants. In addition, she changes the time sheets for Grace and Ric in order to allocate more of their time to camp-related programs and to the specifically funded grants. Previously, all of their time had been charged to the administration and general operating cost grant. Henry was reduced to part-time summer employee, but Nadine allocated some of his time to the specifically funded grants as well.*

## Knowledge check

3. Which is accurate of Happy Campers?

    a. Henry Collins was promoted to camp supervisor.
    b. Ric Alvarez revised the amount of time he charged to the drug and gang programs.
    c. Nadine Henderson charged time for Grace Patel and Ric Alvarez to the specifically funded grant programs.
    d. It was not necessary for Henry Collins to be reduced to a part-time seasonal employee.

# Exercises

1. Do any of the situations described in this case study represent fraud? If so, what situations and what type of fraud?

2. What types of controls might have prevented or detected this situation?

3. What types of other audit procedures might have detected this situation?

Chapter 3

# Case 3: Pledges and Contributions

## Learning objective

- Determine how various board and grantor incentives in a fictitious not-for-profit (NFP) entity may be possible indicators of fraud.

## Before we start

Inherent risk is defined in AU-C section 200, *Overall Objectives of the Independent Auditor and the Conduct of an Audit in Accordance With Generally Accepted Auditing Standards* (AICPA *Professional Standards*), as the susceptibility of an assertion about a class of transaction, account balance, or disclosure to a misstatement that could be material, either individually or when aggregated with other misstatements, before consideration of any related controls. An example of an inherent fraud risk in NFPs could be the incentive to overstate revenues or results in an effort to obtain additional grant funds or contributions from resource providers. Although pledge receivables are not technically "accounts" receivable from a legal and accounting perspective, the indicators of receivable fraud are appropriate "proxies" for indicators of fraud in pledge receivables.

Indicators of receivable fraud could include the following:

- Unexplained differences noted on receivable confirmations received
- Significant or unusual adjustments to receivable records
- Entries made directly to revenue accounts rather than through an integrated subsidiary system
- Amounts deposited that are inconsistent with amounts due
- Significant credit balances in receivable accounts

Another fraud risk inherent in many NFPs receiving contributions is they may feel pressure to misstate functional amounts to maximize program expenses. Additionally, mission-driven board members, directors and employees may be willing to misrepresent amounts in the financial statements in order to appear as if they are providing more program services.

# Background

Paw Patrol is a no-kill animal shelter organized under IRC 501(c)(3). Its primary purpose is to provide forever homes to rescue and shelter animals under their care. The shelter operates in a small cinder block building, which was constructed 40 years ago with volunteer labor and community contributions. Because Paw Patrol is one of only two no-kill shelters in the county, its daily animal population often exceeds the space available. Two years ago, Paw Patrol had to limit its animal population to dogs and cats in an effort to maximize what little space is available.

In addition to operating the shelter, Paw Patrol provides contract animal control services for the county on an as needed basis. They are reimbursed a set fee for each animal rescued regardless of animal size or type or how long it takes to retrieve the animal. County staff prefer to use Paw Patrol over other contractors because they are a no-kill operation.

Paw Patrol has a very good reputation in the area and funds its operations with state and foundation grants, corporate partnership programs, an annual fundraising campaign, contributions, and fees for services. In addition to the fees received from the county for providing animal control services, Paw Patrol charges an affordable fee to new pet owners to cover the cost of shots and care. Several local veterinarians provide pro bono veterinary services when needed. In addition, these veterinarians offer new pet owners a 50% discount on spay or neuter services for their new pets.

The shelter is open seven days a week from 9am to 7pm Monday through Friday, from 9am to 2pm on Saturday and from 1pm to 5pm on Sunday. A full-time executive director is responsible for day-to-day shelter operations, grant writing, fundraising, and community education. In addition to the executive director, the center employs a full-time veterinary technician, a full-time office manager, one part-time receptionist, and a full-time care coordinator. A number of volunteers are scheduled each day to assist in all aspects of the shelter's operations.

The executive director, veterinary technician, and care coordinator rotate providing animal control services for the county. The county provides Paw Patrol with one of its fully equipped animal rescue vans to use for these purposes. In addition, the county provides routine maintenance on the van at no cost to Paw Patrol. Accounting and payroll functions are the responsibility of the office manager.

At its last meeting the board learned an anonymous donor left Paw Patrol $500,000 from her estate for the construction of a new shelter or enhancement of the existing shelter. However, the funds will not be released until Paw Patrol raises a matching $500,000 and the funds revert to the estate if Paw Patrol fails to raise the full $500,000[1]. The board has long wished to enhance its existing shelter but has been hesitant to begin raising funds. With the bequest of $500,000 being conditional and restricted for a new or enhanced shelter, the board is convinced it is now time to begin a capital campaign. The board directs the executive director to develop a fundraising plan for approval at their next meeting.

## Knowledge check

1. Which is accurate of Paw Patrol?

    a. The board authorized the executive director to develop a fundraising plan for their approval.
    b. Paw Patrol is a 501(c)(6).
    c. At a recent meeting, the board of directors postponed a decision to enhance the existing shelter.
    d. The $500,000 anonymous bequest is unconditional.

2. Which is accurate of Paw Patrol?

    a. The shelter is open six days a week.
    b. The executive director is responsible for day-to-day shelter operations, grant writing, fundraising, and community education.
    c. Paw Patrol employs a full-time veterinarian.
    d. No volunteers are used in day-to-day operations.

3. Which is accurate of Paw Patrol?

    a. Paw Patrol operates out of a large brick building.
    b. The primary purpose of Paw Patrol is to provide temporary homes to its animal population.
    c. Paw Patrol is the only no-kill shelter in the county.
    d. Two years ago, Paw Patrol had to limit its animal population to dogs and cats.

## The case

*The following discussion takes place the morning after the board meeting between executive director, Cassandra (Cass) Pursley, veterinary technician (vet tech), Lacey Kendrick, and office manager, Florence Burns.*

"Oh, Cassandra, I am so excited about the $500,000 we are getting to expand this place. My sister-in-law called me last night after her husband got home from the board meeting. Oh my stars, we will be able to start taking in all kinds of animals once we've expanded."

---

[1] Under the requirements of Accounting Standards Update (ASU) 2018-08, *Clarifying the Scope and the Accounting Guidance for Contributions Received and Contributions Made*, issued in June 2018, this is considered a conditional contribution. Paw Patrol is required to raise a matching $500,000 (considered a barrier) and because the estate is not required to disburse the funds if Paw Patrol does not raise the full $500,000 (release of the estate's obligation).

"Hold on there, Florence. The 500K isn't a done deal yet. We have to raise $500,000 to get the bequest money and I'm not sure we will be able to pull off something like that."

"Of course you can do this, Cass. All you need to do is take some of our animals with you when you go begging people for money. I can pick out four right now no one could refuse!"

"That's great, Lacey, but I still need to come up with a plan to raise the money by the next board meeting. You guys may have to cover for me while I work up the plan and the numbers."

"Plan, shman. Let's get cracking on what we could make this place look like. Cassandra, why don't I call the architect who adopted those two beagles last month and see if he can help us with the plans."

"Great idea, Florence. I could meet with him early next week if he's available. As I recall, there isn't anything on my calendar except the obedience classes next Tuesday and Thursday night."

"Hey, Cass. What exactly can we do with this $500,000?"

"I'm not sure of the details, Lacey, but I know it was for a new building or to enhance our existing facility. After a long discussion the board decided it would be too expensive to relocate and construct a new facility, which is why they voted to enhance this one. I can ask the attorney for some details. Why do you ask?"

"I thought we might also be able to upgrade some of our equipment with the money. Our volunteer vets are good about giving us their old equipment, but it would be nice to have something state-of-the-art or at least new."

"Good point, Lacey. I'll ask the attorney about this as well. In the meantime, why don't you see if there are any state grants out there for equipment? I know in the past I've had a hard time finding grants to replace our existing equipment. Maybe funding is different when it's new equipment for new facilities."

"I'll get on this sometime in the next week. Ah, here comes our first potential forever owner. Looks like it's time to get to work."

*Over the next week Cass meets with the architect, Hui Yin Miller, who agrees to offer her design and project oversight services pro bono. Hui Yin tells Cass she can have several designs and the estimated cost of each for her review in the next two weeks. After meeting with the architect, Cass calls Lacey and Florence into her office.*

"Florence, your idea to call Hui Yin was nothing short of brilliant. She agreed to do all the design and project oversight for us at no cost. I'm going to find it hard to wait two weeks to see the plans she promised to have for me."

"This is wonderful news Cassandra. I could tell when she walked out of here with two beagles instead of the one she planned on she was a good woman."

"Have you had any luck with the fundraising plan, Cass?"

"Not really, Lacey. Until Hui Yin gives me a number, I can't really get too deep into the planning but for right now I'm going to use $1,000,000 for our cost. That reminds me, Florence. I need you to give me a list of the folks who have given us any amount of money over the last 10 years or so. Also, are there any records of the folks who provided funding for the shelter all those years ago?"

"The 10-year list won't be too hard because I always do an annual summary of contributions for the auditors. Getting information on the original donors may be a bit more challenging. Don't worry, I have connections and I don't mind using them."

"Thanks, Florence. On another note, Lacey, have you had any luck finding grant money for new equipment?"

"I haven't had time yet, Cass, but I will get to it soon. I had plenty of time to think about all kinds of things last night since I stayed over to watch the afghan we rescued yesterday. She was in really bad shape. Some people should be outlawed from owning a pet, you know?"

"Lacey, I wish you had said something because I could have taken a shift watching her. What were some of the things you thought about last night when you couldn't sleep?"

"Well, I hate to look a gift horse in the mouth, but if we expand our capacity we're going to need a lot more money for operations. More animals equal more food, toys, and supplies not to mention more work for our volunteers. We already have to stretch to make ends meet and I'm worried about how we will find the additional funds."

"Lacey, child, you worry too much. Let's cross that bridge when we come to it, all right?"

"Sure, Florence Sunshine."

*Two weeks later, Hui Yin Miller gets the designs and cost estimates to Cassandra and Florence gets her the 10-year donor information. Cassandra spends the next week developing a fundraising plan and a construction timeline, which she discusses with board chair, Paul Slater, before the next board meeting.*

"You've done some really great work here, Cassandra. What a coup to have gotten Hui Yin Miller to do her work pro bono. She's one of the best architects in the region and I'm looking forward to working with her."

"I thought I would invite her to the board meeting next week if it's all right with you, Paul."

"Another great idea, Cassandra. Let's look at the designs and costs Hui Yin did for us. Oh no, I can tell by the look on your face you're not happy."

"It's not that I'm not happy. I'm disappointed all of the cost estimates are more than what I think we can raise, which means we will have to 'settle' and I don't like having to 'settle,' Paul."

"I hear you, Cassandra, but sometimes you have to do some adulting, which may mean you have to 'settle' on this project. Remember, if you don't want to 'settle' then you need to work a little harder and raise some more money."

"I know, Paul, and I get it, but I still don't like it."

*During the board meeting, the board decides not to "settle" for something less than what they believe the shelter needs. As a result, Cassandra will need to raise a total of $650,000 to meet the conditions of the $500,000 bequest and to make the enhancements the board approved. In addition, the board voted to kick off the fundraising campaign by the end of the next month with a goal of starting construction when one-half of the funds ($325,000) has been raised in cash. The board directed Cassandra to have all the money raised and the construction complete in the next 18 months.*

"I'd like to thank the board for their support of this project and the trust you have put in me to get things done in the next 18 months. I've never done a capital campaign before but the staff and I are up to the challenge. To get things started, I brought each of you a pledge card to allow you to put *your* money where *your* mouth is. Remember you can pay it all up front or over the next three years, but we really need your money up front if possible. You want to start construction when we have half of the goal in cash, which means the sooner you pay, the sooner we can start building our dream shelter."

"Sneaky move, Cassandra."

"Thanks, Paul. Within the next week I will be sending all of you your contact list and fundraising goals. I know I don't need to remind you it will take a lot of hard work from all of us to raise the $650,000."

"What's the overall goal again for us board members, Cassandra?

"Paul, the plan is for the board to 'give or get' $450,000 which, when spread among the 20 of you, shouldn't be too difficult. Most of you are well-connected in this community and will be able to access those connections for something besides their annual operating contribution. The staff and I will be scrambling to raise the other $200,000."

*In total the board members pledge $100,000 toward the facility enhancements with payment to be made in the next six months.*

*The next day Cassandra meets with Lacey, Florence, and care coordinator, Ed Morrison, to show them the plans and to explain the campaign goals and timeline.*

"Wow, Cass. This will be quite the facility when everything is complete. I can't believe the board voted to go all out with the enhancements. I really can't believe I need to raise $50,000 to help do it either!"

"I can't believe the board went all out and left us poor working stiffs to raise $200,000! All my friends and neighbors drink Natty Lite, Cass. How am I going to get $25,000 out of folks like these?"

"Calm down, Ed. You don't have to limit yourself to your friends and neighbors. Go after some of the suppliers we use and sell them on the idea. The file I gave you has a lot of ideas for raising the $25,000 and a few contacts to get you started."

"Lacey, you and I will be looking for grants to help with some of what we have to raise. I'm sorry the $650,000 doesn't include enough to get all the equipment you want. Think positive. If we raise more than the $650,000 I'm sure the board wouldn't object to using the additional money to invest in equipment."

"I don't want to be a wet blanket or anything, Cassandra, but if we tap all our resources and use all of our time raising money for the facility, when will we have time for the operating campaign? It's scheduled to kick off in three months and I'm worried folks won't have money to give to both."

"To be honest, Florence, I'm a little worried about this, too. I'm putting you in charge of getting some collection jars made and putting them in as many stores as will take them. Make sure you clearly state on the labeling the money will go to support our operations. This way we will have at least a few coins for operations next year!"

*When leaving the meeting, Florence mutters:*

"I need to raise a lot of money before we can make this shelter what it needs to be, but we *have* to get the money for all the poor puppies and kittens out there. I need to think about this because I will not let Cassandra fail. It would kill her to have to let go of this dream."

*Over the next five months, the board, staff, and volunteers of Paw Patrol conduct the fundraising campaign and the annual operating campaign. To date, they have raised $550,000 of the $650,000 goal for the shelter expansion and collected over one-half of the pledged amounts. Many donors chose to pay their contribution in full when they heard construction would begin when half of the funds were collected. As a result, Paw Patrol collected $350,000 from donors in addition to the $500,000 bequest.*

*The following conversation occurs at the groundbreaking ceremony between board chair, Paul Slater; architect Hui Yin Miller; and, executive director, Cassandra Pursley.*

"I don't mind admitting this to you, Paul, but when the board approved this project and set the timeline, I wasn't sure we would make it."

"Since we're being honest, Cassandra, I have to admit I'm surprised at how quickly we raised the funds as well. I know you were concerned about the timeline, but I knew this community would come out and support us. Sometimes when you're adulting you have to have a little faith."

"Point taken, Paul. Look, there's Hui Yin Miller. I'm going to go over and say hi."

"I'll join you, Cassandra."

"Hello there, Paul, Cassandra. This is quite the event you have going on here. I especially loved seeing the St. Bernard bring the shovel out for the groundbreaking. Whose idea was it anyway, Cass?"

"The idea was all Lacey's. She's the vet tech who helped you with adopting Mutt and Jeff. She works with all our animals to teach them tricks and loves every minute of it. Well, Hui Yin, you're about to be earning your keep now construction is starting. By the way, I can't thank you enough for finding us a contractor who was willing to get paid when we got paid. I know this is my first capital campaign, but I don't think what they are doing is standard operating procedure."

"Probably not, Cassandra, but the owner is a friend of mine and he was more than willing to help you with this project. We had him over to the house the other night and he had a chance to meet Mutt and Jeff.

Needless to say, it was love at first sight. I wouldn't be surprised if you don't see him one day soon looking for his own shelter dog, or dogs!"

"We would love it, Hui Yin. I'll talk to you again next week to work out all the construction start details."

"Sure thing, Cassandra."

*The next day the following conversation takes place in the office between Florence and Ed Morrison, care coordinator.*

"Hi there, Ed. How are things going?

"Pretty good, Florence. I brought the pledge cards in for those contributions I told you about a few weeks ago."

"Good thing, Ed, because I was about to have to go all collection agency on you. We were so close to the goal and getting the bequest money that I included your pledges in my reports to Cassandra. Normally I wait to get the supporting paperwork, but Cassandra really needed a pick-me-up. I figured 'what the heck,' Ed's good for these and added them to our totals. The look on her face when I told her we had met the $500,000 matching requirement was absolutely priceless."

"I wish I had been here to see it, Florence, but I'm really glad I was able to take a tiny bit of the pressure off of her."

*Looking at the pledge cards, Florence says:*

"These two pledges for $5,000 each take off more than a tiny bit of pressure, Ed. Wow, all of these pledges are for at least $1,000 each. You did a great job after Cassandra gave you a push at the staff meeting last month. It seems your Natty Lite friends and those contacts Cassandra gave you really came through for us."

"It really wasn't too hard once I set my mind to it. All of us know how important the expansion is to our furry friends. Or not-so-furry friends like the two poodles I rescued yesterday."

"I know, Ed. When you brought those two in yesterday I cried for 10 minutes. Who would do such awful things to any animal, much less man's best friend?"

"Making the world a safer place for these critters is what keeps me coming to work every day. See you later, Florence."

*Two weeks later Lacey rushes into Cassandra's office waving a sheaf of papers.*

"Cass, Cass. I found it and it's everything we've been looking for all in one grant."

"What is it Lacey? A million-dollar contribution with no strings?"

"I wish. It's good but not that good. Remember how I was concerned with how we were going to make things work once we were taking in more animals?"

"Sure, I do because it worries me, too. Did you find a solution?"

"It sure looks like one. I found this state grant, which provides seed money to new businesses to start their business or to existing businesses for expansion. We may be a not-for-profit, but I figured we were still a business. According to the person I talked to at the state, we would be considered a business and our expansion project could qualify for funding. The grant funds have to be used to fund operating costs associated with the business expansion, which is exactly what we need. If we qualify, we could get up to $100,000 a year for three years to cover the additional operating costs."

"This is wonderful news, Lacey. What's the catch?"

"Why do you always think there's a catch, Cass?"

"I've been doing a lot of adulting lately and it's made me a lot more skeptical about things, especially when they sound too good to be true."

"You're right, there is a catch. The money is only available in this grant cycle and it's only available for projects that are complete at the time of the grant application."

"How does this fit in with our timetable?"

"The grant funding cycle is the state's fiscal year, which ends in June. This means we would have to have at least a certificate of occupancy by June 30, which is less than nine months away."

"Oh Lacey, I don't see how we could possibly have the expansion done by then. We only broke ground two weeks ago and construction isn't expected to be complete for another 15 months. The contractor is giving us a great deal on the price and the payment schedule, which we agreed to in exchange for the project taking longer."

"Isn't there some way to push the contractor, Cass? Maybe you could agree to pay them faster or something. Then they could work faster on our project."

"It's something to think about, Lacey. I'll reach out to the contractor today."

*Before calling the contractor, Cassandra meets with Florence to discuss the status of the fundraising efforts, collections, and how the operating campaign is going.*

"Florence, last night I was looking at the spreadsheets you gave me, and I want to make sure I'm interpreting the numbers correctly. Although I am ecstatic about the success of the capital campaign, it appears our operating campaign has suffered quite a bit."

"You may remember this was something we all talked about when the project was first approved. We are seeing a bit of a drop off in our operating campaign but I'm sure we'll make it up before the end of the year."

"I appreciate your optimism, Florence, but year-end is less than three months from today. It looks as if we are only at 25 percent of our operating campaign goal when we are usually at 50 percent at this point in the campaign. How are those collection jars in the stores doing, by the way?"

"It's funny because I thought those would be a great way to collect operating funds. They're locked to prevent a customer or store employee from taking the cash and I have Donna pick them up every week."

"Who is this Donna person, Florence?"

"Oh, she's this great lady who is in my Bunco group. She moved here a few months ago from someplace out west, I think. She wanted to get involved in the community and I told her we could use her here at the shelter and she has been the best worker. She jumped right in and volunteered to pick up the collection jars for me. I let her have the master key and she counts out everything and gives me a summary of the collections by store. She even takes the deposit to the bank for me. If it weren't for her, I wouldn't have had the time to work on the capital campaign."

"Are you sure we can trust her, Florence?"

"Well, I thought we could. What are you trying to say, Cassandra?"

"I don't know, Florence, but it seems she has a lot of access to our cash and we don't really know her."

"I know her, Cassandra, and I trust her. Maybe I'll start picking up those jars and Donna can help me count the money and get the deposit ready. I'll still let her take the deposit to the bank because it really saves me a lot of time."

"I think this would be best, Florence."

*Leaving, Florence says to herself:*

"Well, if she doesn't trust Donna I'm sure glad I didn't tell her my suspicions about Ed's pledges. She would be devastated if she knew three of his donors don't seem to exist. I think I'll keep this to myself for now. If I'm honest, she probably wouldn't be too proud of how I've been coding operating campaign money as capital campaign money, either."

*Later in the week Cassandra calls the contractor, Roger Helms, to discuss the possibility of moving up the construction completion date.*

"I know you're doing us a huge favor on the project, Roger, but I need to ask you if there is any way we can move up the completion date."

"The thing is, Cass, I scheduled my crews assuming the current project timeline. Most of the subs agreed to take less for their work because they love your mission over there at Paw Patrol. The tradeoff for them was feeling good but also using the slower timetable to work in other jobs. If I speed things up, they'll take a hit financially."

"Oh, I didn't realize all the moving parts our deal has. You were kind enough to agree to let us pay you when we collected our pledges but what if we could pay you what you need to cover your costs every month? Would you be able to help the subs with their finances if we did this, Roger?"

"This would certainly give them an incentive to stay on your job instead of working other jobs. Tell you what, let me talk to them and see what they think."

"Sounds good, Roger."

*A few days later Roger calls Cassandra to let her know the subs are willing to work more on the Paw Patrol project as long as they can get paid every month for their actual costs. Cassandra goes to see Lacey in her office.*

"All right, Lacey. The contractor has agreed to move up the completion date, but it is going to be very tight."

"What did you do Cass? Don't get me wrong, because this is great news, but I'm still curious as to how you made things work."

"What's this, Lacey, a little adulting for you, too?"

"You told me you were learning to question things when they sounded too good to be true. I'm simply throwing this adulting thing back at you, Cass."

"All right, all right. I had to agree to pay them every month based on the costs they incur instead of paying them whenever we collected on our pledges."

"Oh Cass. Are you sure about this? We can always keep looking for grants to help with our operating expenses."

"No, Lacey. We need to go for this grant. I met with Florence the other day and our operating campaign is basically in the basement. One thing I've learned from our board chair these last few months is to have faith and that's what I'm doing now. In fact, I'm taking a huge leap of faith here, Lacey. Go ahead and apply for the grant and I'll somehow find the cash flow to pay Roger every month."

"All right, Cass, but only if you're sure."

---

## Exercises

1. Are there any potential fraud risks in this case? If so, what are they?

2. What type of controls might have prevented/detected these situations?

3. What type of audit procedures might be considered in this situation?

---

Chapter 4

# Case 4: Overtime Fraud

## Learning objectives

- Identify how personnel policies and procedures in a fictitious not-for-profit entity (NFP) can be circumvented and lead to possible fraud or abuse.

- Determine the importance of understanding the environment in which a fictitious NFP entity operates and how it may affect the development and execution of personnel policies and procedures.

## Before we start

In many NFP entities, salaries and benefits represent the major natural expense category. Employees of NFPs are often paid less than their counterparts in the private sector which may lead some employees to rationalize misappropriation of assets as compensation for their low salary levels. Additionally, work force reductions or reduced hours in times of limited resources may create an unstable work environment. These circumstances may pressure employees to work a second job while "on the clock" of their NFP employer. Low pay, reduced hours, and increased work load often create incentives for employees to misappropriate assets by recording time not actually worked for the benefit of their NFP employer.

Payroll and personnel controls, and therefore audit procedures, typically focus on the accuracy of the amounts paid (paid for actual hours worked at approved rate of pay) as indicated on the manual or electronic time records and documented in an employee's personnel file. In some a NFPs employees may not work a standard 40-hour 8am to 5pm/Monday through Friday work week.

Controls relating to time worked do not often focus on the legitimacy of hours worked outside the regular work day or work week. In NFPs, the approval of an employee's supervisor may be the only evidence the time worked is legitimate. Unfortunately, the supervisor may not be personally aware of whether the employee actually worked the hours indicated on the time record.

# Background

Eliminate Hunger is a 501(c)(3) organization whose mission is to eradicate hunger in its service area. To this end, Eliminate Hunger operates a large regional food bank and nine collection centers located throughout the three counties. The service area encompasses the three counties comprising the metropolitan statistical area (MSA).

Nonperishable food items are delivered to local food pantries, shelters, churches, schools and other organizations serving persons in need of food from the food bank's collection and distribution center. Deliveries are made daily Monday through Saturday to the larger participating organizations and weekly Monday through Friday to the smaller participating organizations.

Eliminate Hunger employs 12 qualified drivers with a current commercial driver's license (CDL) to pick up food at the collection centers and deliver food to the participating organizations. Part-time employees or trained volunteers accompany the drivers at all times. All trucks were purchased with federal or state grant funds. A grant from the State Department of Transportation (DOT) helps offsets truck maintenance costs.

The majority of funding for Eliminate Hunger comes from grants received from federal and state departments of agriculture, transportation, and health and human services. Additional funds are obtained through an annual fundraising campaign, a twice-yearly fundraising dinner, and an endowment established at the local community foundation.

The organization has been in existence 50 years and has a high demand for its services. Even though the unemployment rate in the MSA is moderate, individuals with a CDL are in high demand and Eliminate Hunger is often understaffed. The six weeks needed to process an applicant's application and conduct the necessary health screening and background investigation often exacerbate the understaffed situation. In some cases, volunteers who have been previously screened and investigated are used to fill in when the organization is understaffed. In the past five years, Eliminate Hunger has incurred a significant amount of overtime due to the understaffed situation.

Each collection location is staffed with a full-time supervisor and a part-time assistant. All other employees work out of the main office in the collection and distribution center. The executive director has been with Eliminate Hunger 40 years and both the director of operations (DOO) and the chief financial officer (CFO) have been with the organization more than 10 years. Volunteers are scheduled to work at the collection centers and at the collection and distribution center each week.

# Knowledge check

1. Which is **not** accurate of Eliminate Hunger?

    a. The unemployment rate is low and individuals with a CDL are in low demand.
    b. Eliminate Hunger's mission is to eradicate hunger in its service area.
    c. The service area encompasses the three counties that make up the metropolitan statistical area.
    d. Eliminate Hunger has been in existence for 50 years.

# The case

Due to a five-year mandatory auditor rotation policy, a new audit firm was recently selected to replace the former firm which provided audit services to Eliminate Hunger during the last five years. All policies and procedures have been provided to the new auditor for review. Following these reviews, the engagement in-charge, Samantha Eller, prepared this summary of Eliminate Hunger's payroll procedures.

| Eliminate Hunger<br>Payroll procedures manual excerpts |
| --- |
| All employees are paid every other Friday based on the time worked in the previous full two-week period. |
| All employees (exempt and hourly) complete a bi-weekly hard copy time sheet. For hourly employees, a time card supports the time worked on the time sheet. By signing the time sheet, employees indicate the total and type of hours worked are true and correct. |
| Employees working for more than one program, division, or department allocate the total time spent to each program, division, and department on the face of their time sheets. |
| An employee's immediate supervisor signs his or her time sheet indicating approval of the regular and overtime hours worked. |
| Overtime is to be kept to a minimum and only incurred when it is necessary to provide unexpected after-hours deliveries. All overtime is to be approved by an employee's immediate supervisor. |
| Departments and divisions within Eliminate Hunger submit complete and signed time cards to the payroll department by noon every other Monday. |
| Payroll department personnel verify the math accuracy of each time sheet and ascertain it has been signed by the employee and his or her supervisor. The payroll clerk enters the information from the time sheet into the payroll system for processing. |

# Knowledge check

2. Which is accurate of Eliminate Hunger's payroll procedures?

    a. The payroll clerk enters the information from the time sheet into the payroll system for processing.
    b. Payroll department personnel do not ascertain that time sheets have been signed by the employee.
    c. Payroll department personnel do not ascertain that time sheets have been signed by the employee's supervisor.
    d. All overtime is approved by an employee's supervisor before it is worked.

3. Which is accurate of Eliminate Hunger's payroll procedures?

    a. Payroll personnel do not verify the math accuracy of each time sheet.
    b. All overtime is to be approved by an employee's immediate supervisor.
    c. Overtime is encouraged.
    d. Only overtime incurred on weekends is required to be approved in advance by an employee's supervisor.

*As part of the preliminary audit planning, Samantha Eller obtains interim financial statements from the CFO for Eliminate Hunger, Stephan Gonzalez. She also obtains the year-to-date program budget reports. From this information, Samantha concludes, among other things, payroll and benefits are a significant expense for Eliminate Hunger.*

*At the engagement brainstorming session, payroll and benefits and gifts-in-kind are identified as potential fraud risks and a number of preliminary audit procedures are identified as being necessary.*

*The following conversation takes place between the engagement in-charge, Samantha Eller, and Stephan Gonzalez, the CFO.*

"Stephan, I am not sure how much time your former auditors spent with you discussing potential areas where fraud might occur. My firm makes it a standard audit procedure to talk to an organization's CFO about where they think fraud might occur in their organization. Where do you think you might be subject to fraud here at Eliminate Hunger?"

"I am glad you asked me this, Samantha, because our former auditors talked only to the CEO and board chair about these types of things. I think one of the areas we may be at risk for fraud is in our procurement of truck maintenance and related supplies. We are a pretty small shop when you ignore our food collections and disbursements. As such, we have a number of areas where we are challenged with properly segregating duties and the truck maintenance function is one of those areas. Compounding the loosely segregated duties is no one around here knows what most of the things we buy are. Most of the time we all kind of take Russell's word on things."

"Are you referring to Russell Parker the transportation supervisor?"

"Yes, sorry. I keep forgetting you are the new auditor on the block and may not know all of our folks yet."

"No problem, Stephan. It sounds as if truck maintenance would be a good area for us to review. After food stuffs, what would you say is your biggest line item expense?"

"This is a no-brainer, Samantha. Payroll, and of course the related benefits, are our biggest expenses. I recognized this early in my career here and have established what I think are some pretty strong controls."

"Do you think you are at risk for any payroll fraud, Stephan?"

"I don't really think we are. Our hiring process is pretty tight what with the background and CDL checks. These make me pretty sure we are not at risk for any fictitious employees."

"Looking at those financial statements you gave me I noticed there is a significant amount of overtime in this organization. From what I could tell, most of the overtime is incurred by the drivers. Why is that, Stephan?"

"Right now there is a strong demand in this area for commercial drivers which has driven up salaries. We are not able to compete with the salaries the private sector is paying drivers, or most any other position for that matter. Believe it or not, when I started here 10 years ago we had drivers knocking on our door and begging us for a job."

"I understand not being able to offer salaries competitive with the private sector. It is a challenge all of our not-for-profit clients face. Why does this affect your overtime, though?"

"Well, Samantha, because we don't offer competitive wages, very few drivers apply for our positions. A small applicant pool means it takes us longer to fill vacant positions. To meet our scheduled pickup and delivery times, we assign specific routes to our drivers and when we are down a driver, those routes are spread among our current drivers."

"I can see where this would be challenging, Stephan. It probably doesn't help you deliver six days a week and sometimes after hours."

"You're right there, Samantha. Tight labor market, low wages, long vacancy periods, and collection and delivery commitments are what's creating the overtime situation."

"I've looked over your payroll procedures and they are pretty strong. However, what do you do to make sure drivers are actually working when they say they are?"

"Unfortunately, Samantha, our control here is the supervisor's approval on the driver's time sheet which is supposed to mean the hours worked are accurate. Honestly, I don't know how Russell could really know if the driver worked or not unless he is riding along with them."

"Stephan, are the drivers required to have Russell approve the overtime before they work the hours? I realize this might not always be possible or efficient but it might better support the legitimacy of the hours on their time sheet?"

"I'm not sure what our policy is. but Russell might have something informal in place."

"Thanks Stephan. Could you set me up to see Russell later today? I would like to get some more information from him about his purchasing and the overtime approval process."

*Later, at the meeting with in-charge Samantha Eller and transportation supervisor, Russell Parker.*

"If you don't mind, Russell, I'd like to summarize what you told me to make sure I didn't miss anything or misinterpret anything you said."

"No problem, young lady. Summarize away."

"Uh, all right, Russell. As far as overtime, you don't approve it in advance because the drivers are on the road when they figure out they are running behind and will need to work late. In a sense you approve overtime for the extra routes a driver may be assigned when you make up the weekly schedule . . ."

"I never thought of it like that but it is kind of what I do when I set the schedule."

"But you don't compare the hours on the time sheet to the weekly schedule though."

"No I don't do that but I've got good drivers. A few of them have been here longer than I have and I would trust them with my grandkids' lives."

"Thanks for your time, Russell. I appreciate you making time for me today."

*After discussing her findings with the engagement partner, it is determined payroll, and specifically, overtime is a fraud risk area. Samantha develops additional audit procedures relating to payroll and overtime. Later in the week, the staff auditor assigned to the engagement, DeShawn Moore, asks Samantha to come and look over the results of his payroll test work.*

"Samantha, I'm not sure what any of this means but I wanted to bring it to your attention. Look at the timesheets for these four drivers. They are for different pay periods but each of them has the same amount of regular and overtime hours. This driver here has a route within five miles of the collection and distribution center and this driver has a route going all the way out to the west side of the service area and back. It doesn't make sense they would both have the same amount of overtime. Not only that, but this first driver appears to forget to clock out two to three times each week."

"This is interesting, DeShawn. Look here, did you see this? You have a driver with overtime hours for a Sunday. I know this is the first year we've had the audit, but one thing I learned early on was Eliminate Hunger is adamant their employees have a day to relax and spend time with family. It's why they have an informal 'no working on Sunday' policy."

"You're right. I've seen the sign they put on the door when they leave for the weekend. If they have a 'don't work on Sunday' policy why did Russell approve it?"

"I don't know, DeShawn, but we'll ask him about it. What's the issue with the fourth driver?"

"I hope you don't think I'm crazy, Samantha, but the fourth time sheet is too clean. See how most of the others are smudged or have the corners frayed? Now look at this one. What do you think, Samantha?"

"We'll have to add this to our list of questions, DeShawn. Have you had a chance to work on the disbursements testing yet? After seeing these payroll issues, I wonder if we'll find interesting things in the truck maintenance accounts."

"I only now thought of this, Samantha, but doesn't Russell charge part of his time to the truck maintenance program?"

"Yes he does, DeShawn. What are you thinking?"

"If Russell is approving overtime for the drivers when they didn't actually work it, why wouldn't he do the same with his own time sheet? The operations director would probably have no more idea about Russell working late than Russell does about the drivers and their overtime."

"I see where you're going with this, DeShawn, and I can't say I like it. If, and all of this conversation is a big if, we have overtime fraud with Russell we might also have a compliance issue with the State DOT truck maintenance grant. I am pretty sure he is charging some of his time to the truck maintenance program but I don't know if Stephan picks it up as an allowable cost under the grant."

"Do you think this is the first year for the overtime issues, Samantha? If not, why wouldn't the prior auditors have noticed something?"

"I don't like to speculate about these types of things, DeShawn. Let me contact the manager and partner and see if they want to meet to discuss a new game plan. In the meantime, I'll ask Russell and Stephan about these issues."

"I can talk to Russell if you want. It's always fun to pull the 'wet behind the ears first year auditor and I don't know anything' routine. You would be surprised at how effective this baby face is at getting clients to spill their guts to me."

"Thanks for the visual, DeShawn. I guess it won't hurt to give you first shot at Russell but don't be afraid to call in the cavalry if he doesn't fall for your baby face."

# Exercises

1. How would you resolve the issues presented in this case?

2. Would you consider these situations fraudulent or indicative of abuse?

3. Why do you think the predecessor auditor might not have questioned the overtime hours?

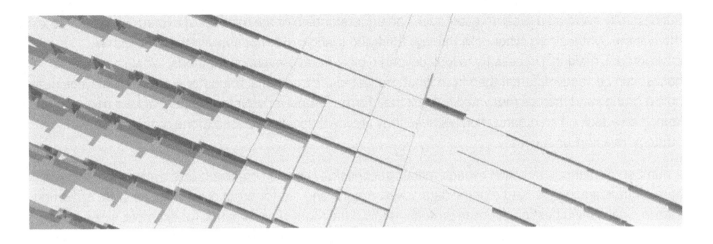

# Chapter 5

# Case 5: Cyber Fraud

## Learning objective

- Identify various types of cyber frauds and their associated risks.

## Before we start

Cyberfraud is becoming more prevalent and more costly every year and is garnering more interest in preventing it and protecting individuals and organizations from it. This is especially important for small- and medium-sized organizations because they typically have fewer controls in place than larger organizations, making them an easy target for a data breach.

According to a survey of cyber claims filed by CPA firms in 2017, 30% of all claims were due to hacking and 31% were due to human error. Social engineering and ransomware accounted for 20% and 10%, respectively, of the claims.[1]

Hackers will continue to test systems for vulnerabilities regardless of the controls an organization might put in place. Additionally, the methods hackers use change rapidly, making cyber controls in place today ineffective tomorrow. However, by implementing adequate data security measures, governmental and not-for-profit organizations may reduce the risk of a data breach or reduce the impact of a successful data breach.

---

[1] *Shore up your data breach detection skills*, Sarah Beckett, Journal of Accountancy, October 2018. Available at www.journalofaccountancy.com.

---

Successfully avoiding a cyber threat requires an understanding of the mindset of cybercriminals and their motivation. Synthesizing cyber risks through the fraud triangle may not apply in the cybercrime environment, making it necessary to look beyond typical fraud prevention methods. What motivates a hacker can be vastly different than from what motivates the traditional fraudster. Former employees may hold a grudge and then be motivated to hack their former employer's system. Other hackers might launch an attack on an organization because they are ideologically opposed to the organization's strategy, mission, or success.

A number of methods by which cybercriminals successfully hack an organization's system are discussed here. Understanding the nature of the data governmental and not-for-profit organizations store is the first step in establishing best practices to protecting this data. Many governments, for example, store credit card and financial institution information. Not-for-profits providing health and human services may store personal financial information as well as health and education related data.

Historically, governmental and not-for-profit organizations invest human, capital, and financial resources in front line services and mission-oriented activities rather than internal control systems. Similarly, they often make minimal or inadequate investments in technology and devote little or no resources to cybersecurity. As such, hackers find governmental and not-for-profit organizations easy targets for a cyberattack. There are, however, some controls all governmental and not-for-profit organizations, regardless of size, can implement to reduce their vulnerability to a cyberattack. These include the following:

- Train users on security practices by regularly educating employees about new attacks and risks
- Create and test system backups ensuring backups are consistent with the recovery time defined in the organization's disaster recovery plan
- Prioritize anti-virus and security patches on all systems in a timely manner
- Implement network segmentation controls that consider which individuals/functions need access to which systems and data
- Review existing insurance policies for adequacy of cyber coverage
- Create a written incident response plan to help lessen the impact of a breach should one occur
- Monitor logs from firewalls, anti-virus programs, etc.[2]

Governmental and not-for-profit organizations need to get in front of cybersecurity risks and the hackers who prey on their vulnerable systems. Best practices which can minimize vulnerability to hackers include the following:[3]

- Encrypting sensitive data and full disk encryption on all relevant equipment including mobile devices and external storage
- Using a multi-factor or two-factor authentication (known as 2FA) system for remote access
- Establishing strong controls over cloud and vendor management systems
- Performing security awareness training for all employees on a regular basis
- Including internal security controls on embedded devices such as web cameras, door badge access systems, and HVAC systems

---

[2] *Why cyberdefenses are worth the cost.* Mark Shelhart, Journal of Accountancy. November 2018.

[3] Based on the article *Inside the Mind of a Hacker: Knowing the Motivations Can Help You Mitigate the Risk of a Breach.* By Stan Sterna, JD and Nick Graf, CISSP, CEH, CIPT published in the Florida CPA Today Fall 2018 edition.

- Documenting and testing incident response plans
- Implementing a formal data retention policy, which includes processes for the secure deletion of data
- Protecting the physical security of all relevant equipment both onsite and offsite
- Conducting annual penetration tests and investigating and correcting issues identified

## What is a data breach?

A *data breach* occurs when someone gains access to information that contains confidential information. This can occur because of a lack of security, the bypassing of security, or the elimination of security. Data breaches occur when information is stolen from computers and other electronic devices. Data breaches can also occur when devices containing information are lost or misplaced. Data breaches usually fall under one of the following types:

- Outsiders
- Insiders
- Accidental loss
- State sponsored

Data breaches not only inconvenience the victim companies and individuals whose information has been compromised, but they also place a significant cost on the victim. Because an organization is considered to be negligent in its duties to safeguard the information provided to it by employees, donors, customers, and others, there is a significant cost to being a victim of a data breach.

## Cyber frauds

*Cyber fraud* and *cybercrime* are terms used to identify illegal activities involving the Internet and the use of computers or other electronic devices. Cybercrime is one of the greatest threats facing our country and has enormous implications for our national security, economic prosperity, and public safety. The range of threats and the challenges they present for law enforcement expand just as rapidly as technology evolves. Victims of cyber frauds include individuals, businesses, not-for-profits, and government entities.

Cybercrime is evolving and becoming more sophisticated. Cybercriminals now have their own social networks and even have escrow services to protect their interests when conducting transactions with other criminals. Malware can be licensed by criminals, and, if they experience issues, there are tech support teams to assist them with their crimes. Criminals can even rent botnets by the hour for their crime sprees. There is also pay-for-play malware available and an open market for zero-day exploits.[4]

---

[4] See www.knowbe4.com.

# Phishing

*Phishing* is a cybercrime in which the criminals contact the victim through email messages that appear to come from legitimate business or government sources. Often, the email headers are spoofed to make them look legitimate. The purpose of the phishing email is to obtain information such as names, addresses, Social Security numbers, phone numbers, dates of birth, credit card numbers, and other personal information from the victims. When the victims supply the information, the criminals are able to use the information to steal the victim's identity and assets. The following are examples of various types of phishing emails.

| | | |
|---|---|---|
| ◢ | **Date: Today** | |
| | E-ZPass Support | Indebtedness for driving on toll road #00839442 |
| ◢ | **Date: Yesterday** | |
| | E-ZPass Manager | Payment for driving on toll road, invoice #00162217 |
| | District Court | Notice to Appear |
| | FedEx Ground | Unable to deliver your item, #000169181 |
| ◢ | **Date: Last Week** | |
| | FedEx 2Day | Unable to deliver your item, #00000496032 |
| | Boris Attorneys | Inheritance |
| | County Court | Notice to appear in Court #000933926 |
| | State Court | Notice of appearance in Court #0000493961 |
| | Learn Medical Bil... | High demand and good pay in medical billing careers |
| | FedEx 2Day A.M. | We could not deliver your parcel, #00269544 |
| | FedEx 2Day | Courier was unable to deliver the parcel, ID000557896 |
| | m.sourd@mdef5... | Re: 700WFQG |
| | FedEx Internatio... | Unable to deliver your item, #0000374620 |
| | no-reply@discov... | Reminder: $25,000 Discover Personal Loans Video Contest |
| | E-ZPass Agent | Indebtedness for driving on toll road #00678129 |
| | E-ZPass Support | Pay for driving on toll road, invoice #00000371690 |
| | FedEx Internatio... | We could not deliver your parcel, #000729678 |
| | Cash At Home | Local mom makes over $8740 / month! |
| | Technical Support | Webmail Users Maintenance Notice |
| ◢ | **Date: Two Weeks Ago** | |
| | Service Monitor | Alert - Information in your credit report has changed |
| | Passport Renewal | Renew Passport if applicable #12291217 |

## Email example

Thu 6/2/2016 11:43 AM

Invoices Dept <invoices.dept@outlook.com>
The Arizona Society of CPAs Membership Past Due

To    Invoices Dept

Dear CPA:

Our records indicate that your membership fees are past due.

Your privileges as a member of The Arizona Society of CPAs will be terminated if payment is not received by the final due date.

You can download a copy of your invoice at the secure link below.

Invoice422349.pdf

Thank you for your prompt attention to this matter.

Sincerely,

Cindie Hubiak
President / CEO
The Arizona Society of CPAs

--------------------------------------------------

This document and any files transmitted with it are confidential and intended solely for the use of the individual or entity to whom they are addressed. If you have received this email in error, please notify the system manager. This message contains confidential information and is intended only for the individual named. If you are not the named addressee, you should not disseminate, distribute or copy this email.

# Denial of service attacks

*Denial of service attacks* (DoS) occur when criminals use botnets or networks of infected computers to bring down a website or computer system by overloading its capabilities, thus, causing it to crash. In many instances, the criminals follow up on the DoS attack with an attempt to hack the system and upload malware onto the computer while the victim is busy trying to fix the problem.

The most common and obvious type of DoS attack occurs when an attacker "floods" a network with information. When you type a URL for a particular website into your browser, you are sending a request to that site's computer server to view the page. The server can only process a certain number of requests at once, so if an attacker overloads the server with requests, it can't process your request. This is a "denial of service" because you can't access that site. In a distributed denial of service (DDoS) attack, an attacker may use your computer to attack another computer. By taking advantage of security vulnerabilities or weaknesses, an attacker could take control of your computer. He or she could then force your computer to send huge amounts of data to a website or send spam to particular email addresses. The attack is "distributed" because the attacker is using multiple computers, including yours, to launch the DoS attack.[5]

# Brand hacking

This cybercrime occurs when criminals post false or misleading (fraudulent) information on the Internet about a company's products or services or about the company itself. This is usually done via social media websites or blogs. The usual purpose of brand hacking is to tarnish or damage the reputation of

---

[5] Department of Homeland Security, www.us-cert.gov/ncas/tips/ST04-015.

the brand being hacked. Negative ratings on the Internet can steer customers away. A twist on the concept of brand hacking occurred when a hotel chain paid its employees to rate their "roach motel" as a four-star resort on various travel sites, enticing customers with fictitious reviews to get them to stay there.

## Pharming

*Pharming* occurs when a virus or other malicious software is placed on the victim's computer. The malware hijacks the victim's web browser. When the victim types in the website for a legitimate company, usually a bank or financial institution, the malware directs the victim's browser to a fictitious copy of the website set up by the criminal. The criminal is hoping to capture the victim's user ID and password or other useful information. Pharming can also be done by exploiting vulnerabilities on a company's website that allows the criminals to redirect legitimate customers to a spoofed website.

## Spoofing

*Spoofing* is a term used to describe activity that makes a fraudulent website or email look legitimate. The purpose of spoofing is to make the victim believe they are communicating with someone they know, when, in fact, they are providing information to the criminals. It is also common for criminals to spoof phone calls and text messages. The latest FBI data draws on fraud reports submitted by victims around the world from October 2013 to May 2018. In that time frame, the FBI counts 41,058 total U.S. victims who collectively lost at least $2.9 billion.

From October 2013 to May 2018, CEO email fraud collectively cost U.S. businesses at least $2.9 billion.[6] The typical CEO email spoof occurs when criminals send an email to an accounting clerk, bookkeeper, or payables manager that appears to have originated from the CEO of the company. There is usually an invoice attached with instructions to wire or ACH the funds to the vendor as soon as possible. The bank account receiving the funds is usually overseas, or, if it is in the United States, the funds are immediately transferred overseas when they are deposited. Another version of this cybercrime requires the request for copies of payroll records or W-2 and other tax records, giving the criminals access to personal information of the company's employees.

The following illustrates an example of a spoofing email.

---

[6] FBI: Global Business Email Compromise Losses Hit $12.5 Billion. https://www.bankinfosecurity.com/fbi-alert-reported-ceo-fraud-losses-hit-125-billion-a-11206 (retrieved February 28, 2019)

Spoofing example from www.knowbe4.com

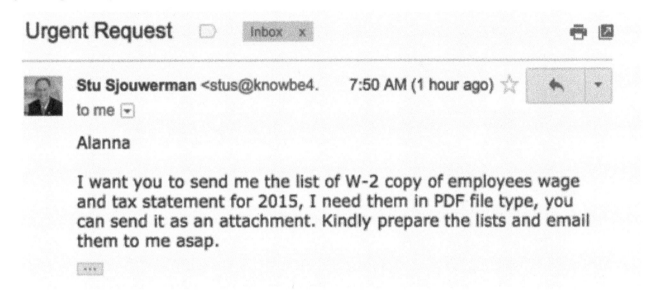

## Knowledge check

1. Phishing is usually conducted with

    a. A cell phone.
    b. An email.
    c. A rod and reel.
    d. A botnet.

# Ransomware

*Ransomware* is a type of malware that is placed on a computer and encrypts all the files on the computer. The criminals then require that the victim pay a ransom in order to obtain the decryption key and gain access to their files again. Well-known examples of ransomware include CryptoLocker and Cryptowall 4.0. Cryptowall 4.0 is the latest version of ransomware being used by many cybercriminals to infect and encrypt all important/ most popular files (such as .xls, .wpd, .ppt, .jpg) on affected computers. Encryption is strong and is impossible to decrypt without paying the ransom (98% of attacks ask for payment to be made in Bitcoin).[7] The FBI estimates that ransomware is a $1 billion a year fraud. The following image illustrates a message that is generated once ransomware has been placed on a computer.

---

[7] See www.thenextweb.com, *Cryptocurrency ransomware payments up 90%, thanks to Ryuk.* Accessed November 6, 2019.

---

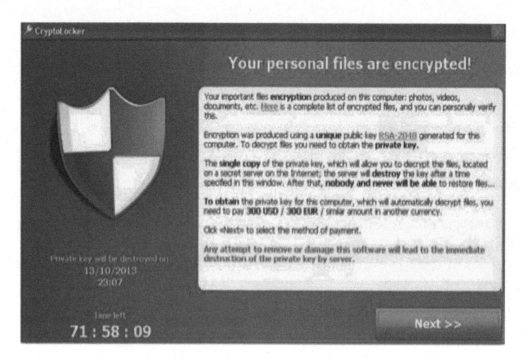

Another type of ransomware, called Reveton, installs itself onto the computer without the user's knowledge. Then, the computer freezes and a bogus message from the FBI pops up on the screen saying the user violated federal law, as shown in the following image. To unlock the computer, the user must pay a fine.[8]

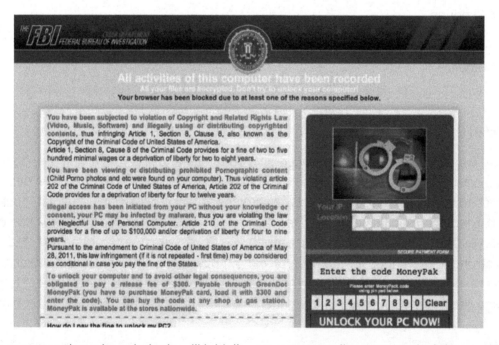

For a single computer, the cybercriminals will initially request a smaller ransom and demand larger ransoms when more computers are infected with the ransomware. Once the deadline for the payment

---

[8] See www.fbi.gov/audio-repository/news-podcasts-thisweek-reveton-ransomware/*view*.

has passed, the criminals increase the ransom demand.[9] According to a cybersecurity company, Coveware, in the first quarter of 2019 organizations paid an average ransom of $12,762 per incident. This is almost double the average amount of $6,733 paid in the fourth quarter of 2018.[10]

Typical ransomware software uses RSA 2048 encryption to encrypt files. Just to give you an idea of how strong this is, an average desktop computer is estimated to take around 6.4 quadrillion years to crack an RSA 2048 key.[11]

On August 9, 2016, the FBI changed its position on paying the Bitcoin ransom to the cyber criminals. Supervisory special agent for the FBI's Cyber Division, Will Bales, said that businesses or individuals targeted by ransomware should refuse to pay the ransom. The U.S. Department of Justice stated there are approximately 4,000 ransomware attacks daily in the United States.

On September 27, 2016, the governor of California signed Senate Bill 1137, making ransomware a form of extortion, even if the victim does not pay the ransom.

Section 523 of the Penal Code[12] is amended to read:

### Chapter 523.

(a) Every person who, with intent to extort any money or other property from another, sends or delivers to any person any letter or other writing, whether subscribed or not, expressing or implying, or adapted to imply, any threat such as is specified in Section 519 is punishable in the same manner as if such money or property were actually obtained by means of such threat.

(b) (1) Every person who, with intent to extort money or other consideration from another, introduces ransomware into any computer, computer system, or computer network is punishable pursuant to Section 520 in the same manner as if such money or other consideration were actually obtained by means of the ransomware.

(2) Prosecution pursuant to this subdivision does not prohibit or limit prosecution under any other law.

(c) (1) "Ransomware" means a computer contaminant, as defined in Section 502, or lock placed or introduced without authorization into a computer, computer system, or computer network that restricts access by an authorized person to the computer, computer system, computer network, or any data therein under circumstances in which the person responsible for the placement or introduction of the ransomware demands payment of money or other consideration to remove the computer contaminant, restore access to the computer, computer system, computer network, or data, or otherwise remediate the impact of the computer contaminant or lock.

(2) A person is responsible for placing or introducing ransomware into a computer, computer system, or computer network if the person directly places or introduces the ransomware or directs or induces another person to do so, with the intent of demanding payment or other consideration to remove the ransomware, restore access, or otherwise remediate the impact of the ransomware.

---

[9] See footnote 4.

[10] See www.zdnet.com, *Ransomware: The cost of rescuing your files is going up as attackers get more sophisticated*, by Danny Palmer. April 16, 2019.

[11] See footnote 4.

[12] See leginfo.legislature.ca.gov/faces/billCompareClient.xhtml?bill_id=201520160SB1137.

# Hacking

*Hacking* is commonly executed by placing malware on a computer system in order to allow the criminals to gain control of the computer or to gain access to information stored on the computer. Currently, computers, cell phones, and other electronic devices are the main target of cybercriminals. As the world is becoming more automated, cybercriminals are increasingly attacking robots and automated production systems in addition to information systems.

A common tool used by cybercriminals is a computer virus. A *virus* is a segment of computer code that attaches itself to a program, such as Microsoft Office, that is already loaded on the computer. A computer virus can cause the infected program to delete, email, or copy files or perform other actions. A computer virus creates copies of itself that it inserts in data files and uninfected programs.

Another common type of malware is known as a *Trojan horse* or *Trojan*. A Trojan is a malware program that is disguised as something else, usually a program or application that the user wanted. Trojans, unlike viruses, are stand-alone programs and do not need to infect a program already installed on the computer. Trojans are often used to load spyware onto infected computers or make them part of a botnet. Trojans often infect computers by piggy-backing on a free program or application downloaded by the user of the device.

A *computer worm* is a type of malware that transmits itself over networks and the Internet and infects any computer connecting with an infected source. Computer worms can be transferred by linking to infected websites. A computer worm is like a Trojan in that it is a stand-alone program that does not need to attach itself to an existing program on the computer. A computer worm can carry a payload such as a ransomware program. The most common payload is a program that installs a backdoor on the infected computer.

Rootkits are another type of malware. A *rootkit* is specifically designed to modify the operating system of an infected computer. The main purpose of a rootkit program is to hide other malware from the user. Because a rootkit program has administrator access, it is not only able to modify the operating system but can also modify any other software installed on the computer. It is difficult to detect rootkits because the rootkit can subvert the software being used to detect the rootkit.

A very dangerous type of malware is known as a *backdoor*. A backdoor allows the cybercriminal unimpeded access to the infected computer, allowing the criminal to bypass the normal authentication processes. A backdoor usually provides the hacker with administrative access to the infected computer.

# Mobile malware

Another method for infecting devices is through a charging station. Cybercriminals load malware onto charging stations located in public places like airports, malls, sports arenas, and subways. Unsuspecting users use their USB ports to connect to the charging stations to recharge batteries in their devices. While they are connected, the data on their devices are copied, and malware is installed.

# Malvertising

Criminals convince ad networks that they are legitimate businesses. The criminals then place ads containing malware on the networks or they link to sites containing malware. The criminals attach malware to ads that appear on legitimate websites so that when the ads are opened the malware is placed on the victim's computer.[13]

# Spyware

*Spyware* is software that tries to gather information about a person or organization without their knowledge or consent and then may send the information to another entity. Spyware may also take control of a computer without the user's knowledge. Some popular versions of spyware for cell phones are as follows:

- HighsterMobile
- Spyera
- Spyrix
- FlexiSpy
- Mobile Spy
- MobiStealth
- mSpy

Popular versions of other types of spyware include the following:

- Keylogger
- Win-Spy
- Spytech Spy Agent
- SpectorSoft
- 007 Spy Software

# Knowledge check

2. Which type of malware attacks an application program that is already installed on the victim's computer?

    a. Rootkit.
    b. Backdoor.
    c. Trojan horse.
    d. Virus.

---

[13] See footnote 4.

# Background

Oceanside was incorporated over 300 years ago and in the last 30 years has grown from a small sleepy village to a bustling beach vacation destination with a vibrant arts community. As the city grew, the increase in tourism provided the city with significant financial resources to invest in human and capital resources. However, over the last five years, it has been challenging for the city's information technology staff to keep up with the ever-increasing pace of technological advances and the proliferation of social media in the business environment.

The city's information technology (IT) department consists of a director and two technology specialists, all of which possess the skills, knowledge, and experience to perform their jobs effectively. Staffing has been considered adequate in the past as the city purchases off-the-shelf software for all applications and contracts with outside specialists if any modifications are needed. Additionally, the finance director and assistant finance director also possess an adequate knowledge of information technology and its role in the city's operations.

Responsibilities of the IT department include the following:

- Administration of the city's intranet and external email functions
- Monitoring employee access to the Internet for appropriateness and applicability to city operations
- Troubleshooting user issues with application software
- Maintenance of IT equipment and hardware (including the city's various servers and cloud-based operations)

# The case

*The following conversation takes place after the weekly meeting of all department heads with the city manager between CFO Anaba Sandoval and IT Director Faisal Shirani.*

"Hey Faisal, I'm going to the AICPA's Government Conference next week and I was trying to decide what sessions to attend and I noticed there are a lot of sessions relating to cybersecurity. What type of topics should I be looking for when deciding which of these sessions to attend?"

"Well, Anaba, as you know cybersecurity is a hot topic these days and means something different to almost everyone. As an IT guy, I probably look at cybersecurity differently than you would, being focused on accounting and such."

"I guess you're right and I know we've had a few discussions in the last year about where my financial management system may be susceptible to a cyberattack but surely you have something to recommend. Faisal, if you have some time now could you walk with me to my office and I can show you the cybersecurity sessions the conference offers?"

"Sure, Anaba, I can look at things and make some suggestions."

*The next week at the AICPA Government Conference, Anaba sees a friend of hers, Abigail Wester, who is the CFO for a large mid-western city.*

"Hey there, Abigail. Imagine running into you at this conference. There must be 1,800 people here and I run into you the first day of the conference."

"You know what they say, Anaba, it is truly a small world. How have you been? It seems as if we haven't seen each other in ages."

"Things are good on the home front as well as at work. Oceanside is still growing, and we are still lucky enough to have significant revenues to cover the cost of our services. How about things with you?"

"Well, the rust belt isn't as lucky as you folks on the coast and we are still facing revenue shortfalls even though the Great Recession has been over for a long time. I'd give anything to be able to fund current services instead of having to look at cutting them every year."

"I know we are lucky Abigail and I'd not want to be in your shoes. Oh no, it's time for my next session."

"Where are you heading, Anaba?"

"Well, at the suggestion of my IT director, I'm sitting in on cybersecurity orientation session. Faisal said it would be good for me to sit in on an overview session before any of the more technical sessions."

"Well girlfriend, great minds think alike because I'm heading to the same session for the same reason! Let's get moving."

*Twenty minutes into the cybersecurity orientation session, Anaba abruptly leaves the session and doesn't return. During the next break, Abigail seeks out Anaba and finds her in the cyber café talking animatedly on her phone. After seeing how agitated Anaba is, Abigail can't help but listen to the conversation.*

"Listen Faisal, I didn't send an email to the city manager asking him to execute a $30,000 wire transfer. I'm telling you like I told Jim, I would never ask him to approve a wire transfer of any amount without discussing it with him in person first."

"Thank goodness Jim contacted me to verify the instructions in the message before he took any action. As soon as I saw the message from him I immediately left my session. Ironically, I was in the cybersecurity overview session you recommended."

"Yes, the message wasn't really written in my style even though it referenced a vendor on our approved vendor list. What I feel like an idiot about is neither Jim nor I noticed his last name was misspelled. I guess when your brain expects to see 'Martin,' it doesn't see 'Marten.'"

"I know, I couldn't believe it either. Who knew Jim would notice the request was to pay a construction contractor for consulting services? I guess his certified transportation planner status is good for more than planning road projects!"

"All right. I'll see you when I get back in the office on Thursday."

*Anaba disconnects from the call and sees Abigail sitting at the station next to her.*

"OK. Spill it Anaba. What is the world is going on with you? I shamelessly listened to your end of the conversation and it sounds like you had some kind of cyber incident."

"Abigail, it was something right out of our session this morning or at least the part of the session I managed to attend."

"Give me the deets and don't leave out anything!"

"Well, you know I left the session soon after it started, and it was because I got a strange email from our city manager. He was asking me why we were paying $30,000 to a construction contractor for consulting services. I had no idea what he was talking about and I left the session to call him."

"Ooh, this sounds like the spoofing thing they discussed in the session after you left."

"Spoofing or loofing, it is scary what happened. The city manager received an email from me from what looked exactly like my city email account but didn't think the wording in it sounded like me. The bank the wire was to be sent to is actually a large regional community bank in our area and the vendor was one we have used before. Jim didn't notice it, but our IT director figured out the spelling of the vendor name in the email was a letter off from the way it is spelled in our approved vendor list – one 'm' instead of two. We are very fortunate the city manager noticed the vendor was a construction company and wondered why we would be paying them for consulting services."

"Wow, Anaba, it sounds like you guys dodged a bullet today. I guess this means you'll be attending all of the remaining cybersecurity sessions!"

"You've got that right, Abigail. I've known cybersecurity was important but having something happen in your own back yard elevates everything to DEFCON 1."

---

## Exercises

1. What type of cyber fraud is represented in this case?

2. Have you or anyone you know been the victim of this type of cyber fraud? If so, what were the factors contributing to the breach? Was the fraud successful? What procedures and/or controls were implemented as a result of the breach?

3. What is your major cyber fraud concern? What are you and your organization doing to addressing cybersecurity concerns?

# Exempt Organizations Glossary

## Governmental terminology

**accounting system.** The methods and records established to identify, assemble, analyze, classify, record, and report a government's transactions and to maintain accountability for the related assets and liabilities.

**accrual basis of accounting.** The recording of financial effects on a government of transactions and other events and circumstances that have consequences for the government in the periods in which those transactions, events, and circumstances occur, rather than only in the periods in which cash is received or paid by the government.

**ad valorem tax.** A tax based on value (such as a property tax).

**advance from other funds.** An asset account used to record noncurrent portions of a long-term debt owed by one fund to another fund within the same reporting entity. (See **due to other funds** and **interfund receivable/payable**).

**appropriation.** A legal authorization granted by a legislative body to make expenditures and to incur obligations for specific purposes. An appropriation is usually limited in the amount and time it may be expended.

**assigned fund balance.** A portion of fund balance that includes amounts that are constrained by the government's intent to be used for specific purposes, but that are neither restricted nor committed.

**basis of accounting.** A term used to refer to *when* revenues, expenditures, expenses, and transfers, and related assets and liabilities are recognized in the accounts and reported in the financial statements. Specifically, it relates to the timing of the measurements made, regardless of the nature of the measurement. (See **accrual basis of accounting**, **cash basis of accounting**, and **modified accrual basis of accounting**).

**bond.** A written promise to pay a specified sum of money (the face value or principal amount) at a specified date or dates in the future (the maturity dates[s]), together with periodic interest at a specified rate. Sometimes, however, all or a substantial part of the interest is included in the face value of the security. The difference between a note and bond is that the latter is issued for a longer period and requires greater legal formality.

**business type activities.** Those activities of a government carried out primarily to provide specific services in exchange for a specific user charge.

**capital grants.** Grants restricted by the grantor for the acquisition or construction, or both, of capital assets.

**capital projects fund.** A fund used to account for and report financial resources that are restricted, committed, or assigned to expenditures for capital outlays, including the acquisition or construction of capital facilities and other capital assets. Capital project funds exclude those types of capital-related outflows financed by proprietary funds or for assets that will be held in trust for individuals, private organizations, or other governments.

**cash basis of accounting.** A basis of accounting that requires the recognition of transactions only when cash is received or disbursed.

**committed fund balance.** A portion of fund balance that includes amounts that can only be used for specific purposes pursuant to constraints imposed by formal action of the government's highest level of decision-making authority.

**consumption method.** The method of accounting that requires the recognition of an expenditure or expense as inventories are used.

**contributed capital.** Contributed capital is created when a general capital asset is transferred to a proprietary fund or when a grant is received that is externally restricted to capital acquisition or construction. Contributions restricted to capital acquisition and construction and capital assets received from developers are reported in the operating statement as a separate item after nonoperating revenues and expenses.

**custodial fund.** A fiduciary fund used to account for financial resources not administered through a trust or equivalent arrangement meeting specified criteria, and that are not required to be reported in a pension (and other employee benefit) trust fund, investment trust fund, or private-purpose trust fund.

**debt service fund.** A fund used to account for and report financial resources that are restricted, committed, or assigned to expenditure for principal and interest. Debt service funds should be used to report resources if legally mandated. Financial resources that are being accumulated for principal and interest maturing in future years should also be reported as debt service funds.

**deferred inflow of resources.** An acquisition of net assets by a government that is applicable to a future reporting period.

**deferred outflow of resources.** A consumption of net asset by a government that is applicable to a future reporting period.

**deficit.** (*a*) The excess of the liabilities of a fund over its assets. (*b*) The excess of expenditures over revenues during an accounting period or, in the case of proprietary funds, the excess of expenses over revenues during an accounting period.

**disbursement.** A payment made in cash or by check. Expenses are only recognized at the time physical cash is disbursed.

**due from other funds.** A current asset account used to indicate an account reflecting amounts owed to a particular fund by another fund for goods sold or services rendered. This account includes only short-term obligations on an open account, not interfund loans.

**due to other funds.** A current liability account reflecting amounts owed by a particular fund to another fund for goods sold or services rendered. This account includes only short-term obligations on an open account, not interfund loans.

**enabling legislation.** Legislation that authorizes a government to assess, levy, charge, or otherwise mandate payment of resources from external resource providers and includes a legally enforceable requirement that those resources be used for the specific purposes stipulated in the legislation.

**encumbrances.** Commitments related to unperformed (executory) contracts for goods or services. Used in budgeting, encumbrances are not generally accepted accounting principles (GAAP) expenditures or liabilities but represent the estimated amount of expenditures that will ultimately result if unperformed contracts in process are completed.

**enterprise fund.** A fund established to account for operations financed and operated in a manner similar to private business enterprises (such as gas, utilities, transit systems, and parking garages). Usually, the governing body intends that costs of providing goods or services to the general public be recovered primarily through user charges.

**expenditures.** Decreases in net financial resources. Expenditures include current operating expenses requiring the present or future use of net current assets, debt service and capital outlays, intergovernmental grants, entitlements, and shared revenues.

**expenses.** Outflows or other consumption of assets or incurrences of liabilities, or a combination of both, from delivering or producing goods, rendering services, or carrying out other activities that constitute the entity's ongoing major or central operations.

**fiduciary fund.** A fund that reports fiduciary activities meeting the criteria in paragraphs 6–11 of GASB Statement No. 84, *Fiduciary Activities*. Financial reporting is focused on reporting net position and changes in net position.

**fund.** A fiscal and accounting entity with a self-balancing set of accounts in which cash and other financial resources, all related liabilities and residual equities, or balances, and changes therein, are recorded and segregated to carry on specific activities or attain certain objectives in accordance with special regulations, restrictions, or limitations.

**fund balance.** The difference between fund assets and fund liabilities of the generic fund types within the governmental category of funds.

**fund financial statements.** Each fund has its own set of self-balancing accounts and fund financial statements that focus on information about the government's governmental, proprietary, and fiduciary fund types.

**fund type.** The 11 generic funds that all transactions of a government are recorded into. The 11 fund types are as follows: general, special revenue, debt service, capital projects, permanent, enterprise, internal service, private-purpose trust, pension (and other employee benefit) trust, investment trust, and custodial.

**GASB.** The Governmental Accounting Standards Board (GASB), organized in 1984 by the Financial Accounting Foundation (FAF) to establish standards of financial accounting and reporting for state and local governmental entities. Its standards guide the preparation of external financial reports of those entities.

**general fund.** The fund within the governmental category used to account for all financial resources, except those required to be accounted for in another governmental fund.

**general-purpose governments.** Governmental entities that provide a range of services, such as states, cities, counties, towns, and villages.

**governmental funds.** Funds used to account for the acquisition, use, and balances of spendable financial resources and the related current liabilities, except those accounted for in proprietary funds and fiduciary funds. Essentially, these funds are accounting segregations of financial resources. Spendable assets are assigned to a particular government fund type according to the purposes for which they may or must be used. Current liabilities are assigned to the fund type from which they are to be paid. The difference between the assets and liabilities of governmental fund types is referred to as *fund balance*. The measurement focus in these fund types is on the determination of financial position and changes in financial position (sources, uses, and balances of financial resources), rather than on net income determination.

**government-wide financial statements.** Highly aggregated financial statements that present financial information for all assets (including infrastructure capital assets), liabilities, and net assets of a primary government and its component units, except for fiduciary funds. The government-wide financial statements use the economic resources measurement focus and accrual basis of accounting.

**infrastructure assets.** Long-lived capital assets that normally are stationary in nature and can be preserved for a significantly greater number of years than most capital assets. Examples of infrastructure assets are roads, bridges, tunnels, drainage systems, water and sewer systems, dams, and lighting systems. Buildings, except those that are an ancillary part of a network of infrastructure assets, are not considered infrastructure assets.

**interfund receivable/payable.** Activity between funds of a government reflecting amounts provided with a requirement for repayment, or sales and purchases of goods and services between funds approximating their external exchange value (also referred to as **interfund loans** or **interfund services provided and used**).

**internal service fund.** A generic fund type within the proprietary category used to account for the financing of goods or services provided by one department or agency to other departments or agencies of a government, or to other governments, on a cost-reimbursement basis.

**investment trust fund.** A generic fund type within the fiduciary category used by a government in a fiduciary capacity, such as to maintain its cash and investment pool for other governments.

**major funds.** A government's general fund (or its equivalent), other individual governmental type, and enterprise funds that meet specific quantitative criteria, and any other governmental or enterprise fund that a government's officials believe is particularly important to financial statement users.

**management's discussion and analysis.** Management's discussion and analysis, or MD&A, is required supplementary information that introduces the basic financial statements by presenting certain financial information as well as management's analytical insights on that information.

**measurement focus.** The accounting convention that determines (*a*) which assets and which liabilities are included on a government's balance sheet and where they are reported, and (*b*) whether an operating statement presents information on the flow of financial resources (revenues and expenditures) or information on the flow of economic resources (revenues and expenses).

**modified accrual basis of accounting.** The basis of accounting adapted to the governmental fund type measurement focus. Revenues and other financial resource increments are recognized when they become both *measurable* and *available to finance expenditures of the current period. Available* means collectible in the current period or soon enough thereafter to be used to pay liabilities of the current period. Expenditures are recognized when the fund liability is incurred and expected to be paid from current resources, except for (*a*) inventories of materials and supplies that may be considered expenditures either when purchased or when used, and (*b*) prepaid insurance and similar items that may be considered expenditures either when paid for or when consumed. All governmental funds are accounted for using the modified accrual basis of accounting in fund financial statements.

**modified approach.** Rules that allow infrastructure assets that are part of a network or subsystem of a network not to be depreciated as long as certain requirements are met.

**net position.** The residual of all other elements presented in a statement of financial position.

**nonspendable fund balance.** The portion of fund balance that includes amounts that cannot be spent because they are either (*a*) not in spendable form or (*b*) legally or contractually required to be maintained intact.

**pension (and other employee benefit) trust fund.** A trust fund used to account for a public employees retirement system, OPEB plan, or other employee benefits other than pensions that are administered through trusts that meet specified criteria. Pension (and other employee benefit) trust funds use the accrual basis of accounting and the flow of economic resources measurement focus.

**permanent fund.** A generic fund type under the governmental category used to report resources that are legally restricted to the extent that only earnings, and not principal, may be used for purposes that support the reporting government's programs and, therefore, are for the benefit of the government or its citizenry. (Permanent funds do not include private-purpose trust funds, which should be used when the government is required to use the principal or earnings for the benefit of individuals, private organizations, or other governments).

**private purpose trust fund.** A general fund type under the fiduciary category used to report resources held and administered by the reporting government acting in a fiduciary capacity for individuals, other governments, or private organizations.

**proprietary funds.** The government category used to account for a government's ongoing organizations and activities that are similar to those often found in the private sector (these are enterprise and internal service funds). All assets, liabilities, equities, revenues, expenses, and transfers relating to the government's business and quasi-business activities are accounted for through proprietary funds. Proprietary funds should apply all applicable GASB pronouncements and those GAAP applicable to similar businesses in the private sector, unless those conflict with GASB pronouncements. These funds use the accrual basis of accounting in conjunction with the flow of economic resources measurement focus.

**purchases method.** The method under which inventories are recorded as expenditures when acquired.

**restricted fund balance.** Portion of fund balance that reflects constraints placed on the use of resources (other than nonspendable items) that are either (*a*) externally imposed by a creditor, such as through debt covenants, grantors, contributors, or laws or regulations of other governments or (*b*) imposed by law through constitutional provisions or enabling legislation.

**required supplementary information.** GAAP specify that certain information be presented as required supplementary information, or RSI.

**special-purpose governments.** Legally separate entities that perform only one activity or a few activities, such as cemetery districts, school districts, colleges and universities, utilities, hospitals and other health care organizations, and public employee retirement systems.

**special revenue fund.** A fund that must have revenue or proceeds from specific revenue sources that are either restricted or committed for a specific purpose other than debt service or capital projects. This definition means that in order to be considered a special revenue fund, there must be one or more revenue sources upon which reporting the activity in a separate fund is predicated.

**interfund transfers.** All transfers, such as legally authorized transfers from a fund receiving revenue to a fund through which the resources are to be expended, where there is no intent to repay. Interfund transfers are recorded on the operating statement.

**unassigned fund balance.** Residual classification for the general fund. This classification represents fund balance that has not been assigned to other funds and has not been restricted, committed, or assigned to specific purposes within the general fund. The general fund should be the only fund that reports a positive unassigned fund balance amount. In other funds, if expenditures incurred for specific purposes exceeded the amounts restricted, committed, or assigned to those purposes, it may be necessary to report a negative unassigned fund balance.

**unrestricted fund balance.** The total of committed fund balance, assigned fund balance, and unassigned fund balance.

# Not-for-profit terminology

**board-designated endowment fund.** An endowment fund created by a not-for-profit entity's governing board by designating a portion of its net assets without donor restrictions to be invested to provide income for a long, but not necessarily specified, period. In rare circumstances, a board-designated endowment fund also can include a portion of net assets with donor restrictions. For example, if a not-for-profit is unable to spend donor-restricted contributions in the near term, then the board sometimes considers the long-term investment of these funds.

**board-designated net assets.** Net assets without donor restrictions subject to self-imposed limits by action of the governing board. Board-designated net assets may be earmarked for future programs, investment, contingencies, purchase or construction of fixed assets, or other uses. Some governing boards may delegate designation decisions to internal management. Such designations are considered to be included in board-designated net assets.

**charitable lead trust.** A trust established in connection with a split-interest agreement in which the not-for-profit entity receives distributions during the agreement's term. Upon termination of the trust, the remainder of the trust assets are paid to the donor or to third-party beneficiaries designated by the donor.

**charitable remainder trust.** A trust established in connection with a split-interest agreement in which the donor or a third-party beneficiary receives specified distributions during the agreement's term. Upon termination of the trust, a not-for-profit entity receives the assets remaining in the trust.

**collections.** Works of art, historical treasures, or similar assets that are (*a*) held for public exhibition, education, or research in furtherance of public service, rather than financial gain; (*b*) protected, kept unencumbered, cared for, and preserved; and (*c*) subject to an organizational policy that requires the proceeds of items that are sold to be used to acquire other items for collections.

**conditional promise to give.** A promise to give that is subject to a donor-imposed condition.

**contribution.** An unconditional transfer of cash or other assets, as well as unconditional promises to give, to an entity or a reduction, settlement, or cancellation of its liabilities in a voluntary nonreciprocal transfer by another entity acting other than as an owner.

**costs of joint activities.** Costs incurred for a joint activity. Costs of joint activities may include joint costs and costs other than joint costs. *Costs other than joint costs* are costs that are identifiable with a particular function, such as program, fund-raising, management and general, and membership development costs.

**donor-imposed restriction.** A donor stipulation (*donors* include other types of contributors, including makers of certain grants) that specifies a use for the contributed asset that is more specific than broad limits resulting from the nature of the organization, the environment in which it operates, and the purposes specified in its articles of incorporation or bylaws, or comparable documents for an unincorporated association. A restriction on an organization's use of the asset contributed may be temporary in nature or perpetual in nature.

**donor-restricted endowment fund.** An endowment fund that is created by a donor stipulation (*donors* include other types of contributors, including makers of certain grants) that requires investment of the gift in perpetuity or for a specified term. Some donors or laws may require that a portion of income, gains, or both be added to the gift and invested subject to similar restrictions.

**donor-restricted support.** Donor-restricted revenues or gains from contributions that increase net assets with donor restrictions (*donors* include other types of contributions, including makers of certain grants).

**economic interest.** A not-for-profit entity's interest in another entity that exists if any of the following criteria are met: (*a*) The other entity holds or uses significant resources that must be used for the purposes of the not-for-profit entity, either directly or indirectly, by producing income or providing services, or (*b*) the not-for-profit entity is responsible for the liabilities of the other entity.

**endowment fund.** An established fund of cash, securities, or other assets that provides income for the maintenance of a not-for-profit entity. The use of the assets of the fund may be with or without donor-imposed restrictions. Endowment funds generally are established by donor-restricted gifts and bequests to provide a source of income.

**functional expense classification.** A method of grouping expenses according to the purpose for which the costs are incurred. The primary functional classifications of a not-for-profit entity are program services and supporting activities.

**funds functioning as endowment.** Net assets without donor restrictions (*donors* include other types of contributors, including makers of certain grants) designated by an entity's governing board to be invested to provide income for generally a long, but not necessarily specified, period.

**joint activity.** An activity that is part of the fund-raising function and has elements of one or more other functions, such as programs, management and general, membership development, or any other functional category used by the entity.

**joint costs.** The costs of conducting joint activities that are not identifiable with a particular component of the activity.

**management and general activities.** Supporting activities that are not directly identifiable with one or more programs, fund-raising activities, or membership development activities.

**natural expense classification.** A method of grouping expenses according to the kinds of economic benefits received in incurring those expenses. Examples of natural expense classifications include salaries and wages, employee benefits, professional services, supplies, interest expense, rent, utilities, and depreciation.

**net assets.** The excess or deficiency of assets over liabilities of a not-for-profit entity, which is divided into two mutually exclusive classes according to the existence or absence of donor-imposed restrictions.

**net assets with donor restrictions.** The part of net assets of a not-for-profit entity that is subject to donor-imposed restrictions (*donors* include other types of contributors, including makers of certain grants).

**net assets without donor restrictions.** The part of net assets of a not-for-profit entity that is not subject to donor-imposed restrictions (*donors* include other types of contributors, including makers of certain grants).

**programmatic investing.** The activity of making loans or other investments that are directed at carrying out a not-for-profit entity's purpose for existence, rather than investing in the general production of income or appreciation of an asset (for example, total return investing). An example of programmatic investing is a loan made to lower-income individuals to promote home ownership.

**promise to give.** A written or oral agreement to contribute cash or other assets to another entity. A promise to give may be either conditional or unconditional.

**underwater endowment fund.** A donor-restricted endowment fund for which the fair value of the fund at the reporting date is less than either the original gift amount or the amount required to be maintained by the donor or by law that extends donor restrictions.

# Single audit and Yellow Book terminology

**attestation engagements.** Attestation engagements concern examining, reviewing, or performing agreed-upon procedures on a subject matter or an assertion about a subject matter and reporting on the results.

**compliance supplement.** A document issued annually in the spring by the OMB to provide guidance to auditors.

**data collection form.** A form submitted to the Federal Audit Clearinghouse that provides information about the auditor, the auditee and its federal programs, and the results of the audit.

**federal financial assistance.** Assistance that nonfederal entities receive or administer in the form of grants, loans, loan guarantees, property, cooperative agreements, interest subsidies, insurance, food commodities, direct appropriations, or other assistance, but does not include amounts received as reimbursement for services rendered to individuals in accordance with guidance issued by the director.

**financial audits.** Financial audits are primarily concerned with providing reasonable assurance about whether financial statements are presented fairly, in all material respects, in conformity with GAAP or with a comprehensive basis of accounting other than GAAP.

**GAGAS.** Generally accepted government auditing standards issued by the GAO. They are published as *Government Auditing Standards*, also commonly known as the Yellow Book.

**GAO.** The United States Government Accountability Office. Among its responsibilities is the issuance of GAGAS.

**OMB.** The Office of Management and Budget. The OMB assists the President in the development and implementation of budget, program, management, and regulatory policies.

**pass-through entity.** A nonfederal entity that provides federal awards to a subrecipient to carry out a federal program.

**performance audits.** Performance audits entail an objective and systematic examination of evidence to provide an independent assessment of the performance and management of a program against objective criteria as well as assessments that provide a prospective focus or that synthesize information on best practices or cross-cutting issues.

**program-specific audit.** A compliance audit of one federal program.

**single audit.** An audit of a nonfederal entity that includes the entity's financial statements and federal awards.

**single audit guide.** This AICPA Audit Guide, formally titled Government Auditing Standards *and Single Audits*, is the former Statement of Position (SOP) 98-3, *Audits of States, Local Governments, and Not-for-Profit Organizations Receiving Federal Awards*. The single audit guide provides guidance on the auditor's responsibilities when conducting a single audit or program-specific audit in accordance with the Single Audit Act, GAGAS, and the Uniform Guidance.

**subrecipient.** A nonfederal entity that receives federal awards through another nonfederal entity to carry out a federal program but does not include an individual who receives financial assistance through such awards.

**Uniform Guidance.** Formally known as Title 2 U.S. *Code of Federal Regulations* Part 200, *Uniform Administrative Requirements, Cost Principles, and Audit Requirements for Federal Awards*. The Uniform Guidance sets forth the requirements for the compliance audit portion of a single audit.

# Index

# REAL FRAUDS FOUND IN NFPS

BY LYNDA DENNIS, PH.D., CPA, CGFO

Solutions

The AICPA publishes *CPA Letter Daily*, a free e-newsletter published each weekday. The newsletter, which covers the 10-12 most important stories in business, finance, and accounting, as well as AICPA information, was created to deliver news to CPAs and others who work with the accounting profession. Besides summarizing media articles, commentaries, and research results, the e-newsletter links to television broadcasts and videos and features reader polls. *CPA Letter Daily*'s editors scan hundreds of publications and websites, selecting the most relevant and important news so you don't have to. The newsletter arrives in your inbox early in the morning. To sign up, visit smartbrief.com/CPA.

Do you need high-quality technical assistance? The AICPA Auditing and Accounting Technical Hotline provides non-authoritative guidance on accounting, auditing, attestation, and compilation and review standards. The hotline can be reached at 877.242.7212.

# Solutions

## Chapter 1

### Suggested solutions to Case 1

1. Elements of the fraud triangle present include the following:

   - There is pressure on location directors to maintain or increase program quality with decreasing funds
   - Opportunity exists at the four offsite locations due to limited staff and oversight
   - Location directors believe the VPO doesn't understand the difficulties they face, which could lead to rationalization of fraudulent transactions

2. Additional procedures that could have been in place to ensure compliance with program requirements, include the following:

   - Review of application files by someone at the administrative office
   - Confirmation of family income using external data bases
   - Surprise visits by the VPO to observe activity during drop off and pick up hours
   - Keep all family files at the administrative office, if in paper form, or limit access to electronic files
   - Periodic review of the waiting list activity and dates of activity

3. Missing or inadequate internal controls include the following:

   - Lacking controls at locations
   - Limited supervision of location directors who are in a position to perpetrate fraud due to limited or missing controls
   - Over-reliance by administrative office leadership on location directors
   - Lack of central oversight or control of program activities and transactions

4. Preliminary audit procedures might include the following:

   - Assessment of locations for potential material fraud
   - Review of controls at all locations
   - Inquiry of selected location personnel at all levels regarding the potential for fraud
   - Review of grant provisions and assessment of related controls over grant transactions

Other audit procedures might include the following:

- Review of files processed by each location
- Sampling selected files from each location to determine validity of applicant name, address, and income level

## Knowledge check solutions

1.

    a. Incorrect. Level Field receives 5% of revenues from fees for program services.

    b. Correct. Level Field is a United Way agency.

    c. Incorrect. Level Field operates in a three-county area.

    d. Incorrect. Level Field receives 80% of its funds from state grants and 15% from community contributions and United Way.

2.

    a. Incorrect. The Human Resources department at the administrative office posts job vacancies, recruits, and performs background checks for location employees.

    b. Incorrect. Level Field uses a cloud-based time management system.

    c. Correct. Operational oversight responsibility is performed by administrative office staff, which are housed in the downtown education/child care facility

    d. Incorrect. Payroll is processed weekly.

3.

    a. Correct. Amanda Miller, Kelly Carter, and Brittany Nelson are teachers at the Downtown location.

    b. Incorrect. Pat Simmons is the director for the South Side location.

    c. Incorrect. Rich Hawkins is the director for the Downtown location.

    d. Incorrect. Ryan Cavanaugh has a cousin who works for a Big Four firm in DC.

# Chapter 2

## Suggested solutions to Case 2

1. The actions of the administrative assistant of Happy Campers, however well intentioned, represent fraud. They have fraudulently represented grant transactions.

2. Controls that might have prevented or detected this situation include the following:

- Implementation of a purchase order system, which would require the approval of, at a minimum, the originator's immediate superior

- Review of purchase orders/invoices by the executive director or a board member (such as the treasurer) for reasonableness of purchase, quantities, and coding
- Review of all work performed by the administrative assistant by the executive director or camp director as appropriate for the work product
- Post payroll review of amounts charged to various cost centers/programs

  Because Happy Campers is a small organization with limited staff, establishing effective controls, such as proper segregation of duties, could prove problematic. As in any organization, any established controls will be ineffective in the case of collusion, which may occur in this case between the camp director and administrative assistant.

3. Audit procedures that might have detected this situation include the following:

- Preliminary inquiries of the executive director and the camp director especially relating to how the administrative and general operating costs previously funded with a state grant were absorbed and/or funded
- Consideration of external environment (that is, reduced state funding for HHS) in light of the organization and the fraud triangle
- Compliance tests of controls (assuming there are properly designed controls in place)
- Review of methodology used to allocate grant costs
- Substantive tests of details
- Tests of program disbursements

## Knowledge check solutions

1.

   a. Correct. Happy Campers has been in existence 30 years.
   b. Incorrect. Happy Campers offers a day program for elementary school age children and half day programs during the school year.
   c. Incorrect. Happy Campers offers half day programs during the school year when there are not classes.
   d. Incorrect. Most of the funding for Happy Campers comes from federal grants.

2.

   a. Incorrect. HHS will not be funding grants for administrative and general operating costs in the next year.
   b. Incorrect. All HHS socio-economic programs will be cut 15% in the next year.
   c. Incorrect. DOJ and the corrections department are the budget winners in the next year.
   d. Correct. HHS will be cutting staff at offices throughout the state in the upcoming year.

3.

    a. Incorrect. Henry Collins was not promoted to camp supervisor. He was reduced to a part time seasonal employee.

    b. Incorrect. Ric Alvarez did not revise the amount of time he charged to the drug and gang programs. Nadine Henderson did this.

    c. Correct. Nadine Henderson charged time for Grace Bennett and Ric Alvarez to the specifically funded grant programs.

    d. Incorrect. It was necessary for Henry Collins to be reduced to a part time seasonal employee

# Chapter 3

## Suggested solutions to Case 3

1. The risk of material financial statement misstatement is present in this case because the organization is involved in fundraising for both capital and operating needs. Specific fraud risks relate to revenue recognition including propriety and classification of pledges as well as the collectability of such amounts. In addition, misappropriation of assets is possible with respect to the collection jars, which are picked up by a volunteer with access to the contents.

2. Controls that might have prevented or detected this situation include the following:

    • Because Paw Patrol is a small organization with limited staff, establishing effective controls, such as proper segregation of duties, could prove problematic
    • Review of all work performed by the office manager by the executive director or another appropriate management-level staff or board member (such as the treasurer)
    • Verification of donor authenticity by someone other than the person soliciting the contribution
    • Review of all capital and operating contribution paperwork by someone other than the originator and/or office manager to ensure proper recording of the amounts

3. Because this is the organization's first capital campaign, the auditor will not be able to compare this year's results with prior efforts. However, results could be compared to industry benchmarks obtained from national (for example, BBB Wise Giving Alliance, and so on) or local organizations. Discussions with board members and client personnel could also help bring light to the matter. Additionally, the auditor might consider confirming a large number of small and large capital and operating campaign contributions directly with donors. For those pledges not confirmed, if felt necessary, the auditor could match donor names and addresses to information in the public domain, including social media. In some cases, the addresses of donors could be matched to community data, employee addresses, prior giving history, and so on. The auditor could also perform analytical and substantive testing on the pledges collected to date and a low percentage could bring attention to the validity of the pledges.

## Knowledge check solutions

1.
   a. Correct. The board did authorize the executive director to develop a fundraising plan for their approval.
   b. Incorrect. Paw Patrol is a 501(c)(3).
   c. Incorrect. At a recent meeting, the board of directors approved, not postponed, plans to enhance the existing shelter.
   d. Incorrect. The $500,000 bequest is conditional upon Paw Patrol raising a matching $500,000.

2.
   a. Incorrect. The shelter is open seven days a week.
   b. Correct. The executive director is responsible for day-to-day shelter operations, grant writing, fundraising, and community education.
   c. Incorrect. Paw Patrol employs a full-time veterinary technician.
   d. Incorrect. Volunteers are used in day-to-day operations

3.
   a. Incorrect. Paw Patrol operates in a small cinder block building.
   b. Incorrect. The primary purpose of Paw Patrol is to provide forever homes to its animal population
   c. Incorrect. Paw Patrol is one of two no-kill shelters in the county.
   d. Correct. Two years ago, Paw Patrol had to limit its animal population to dogs and cats in an effort to maximize what little space is available.

---

# Chapter 4

## Suggested solutions to Case 4

1. At a minimum, additional inquiries are necessary to determine the legitimacy of the noted overtime. The type and extent of additional procedures would depend on the resolution of the noted situations. If legitimate and reasonable, additional procedures may not be considered necessary. In some cases, even though the inquiries indicated the noted overtime was legitimate and reasonable, the auditor might want to review any items in the original sample in greater detail if overtime was paid for the selected item.

2. Responses to this question will vary based on the experience and attitudes of the participants. As presented, the items appear to possibly be fraud or abuse. There is insufficient information in the case to indicate whether or not management override occurred or if the fraud or abuse is material.

---

3. Responses to this question will vary based on the experience and attitudes of the participants. There is insufficient evidence in the case to support definitive answers. However, one reason might be the auditor focused on the controls over payroll rather than the legitimacy of the hours worked. In this case there are no controls over the legitimacy of hours worked other than approval of the time sheet by the supervisor. Another reason might be overtime expense, in the first-year engagement for the predecessor auditor, was consistent with the prior year amount.

## Knowledge check solutions

1.

a. Correct. The unemployment rate is moderate and individuals with a CDL are in high demand.

b. Incorrect. Eliminate Hunger's mission is to eradicate hunger in its service area

c. Incorrect. The service area encompasses the three counties comprising the metropolitan statistical area.

d. Incorrect. Eliminate Hunger has been in existence for 50 years.

2.

a. Correct. The payroll clerk enters the information from the time sheet into the payroll system for processing.

b. Incorrect. Payroll department personnel ascertain that time sheets have been signed by the employee.

c. Incorrect. Payroll department personnel ascertain that time sheets have been signed by the employee's supervisor.

d. Incorrect. Overtime is not required to be approved by an employee's supervisor before it is worked.

3.

a. Incorrect. Payroll department personnel verify the math accuracy of each time sheet.

b. Correct. All overtime is to be approved by an employee's immediate supervisor.

c. Incorrect. Overtime is to be kept to a minimum and only incurred when it is necessary to make unexpected after-hours deliveries.

d. Incorrect. All overtime is to be approved by an employee's immediate supervisor.

# Chapter 5

## Suggested solutions to Case 5

1. The cyber fraud in this case is a legitimate looking but fraudulent email that is sent to the city manager. This type of cyber fraud is spoofing.

2. Responses to this question will vary based on the experience and attitudes of the participants.

3. Responses to this question will vary based on the experience and attitudes of the participants.

## Knowledge check solutions

1.
   a. Incorrect. Vishing is done with a cell phone, not phishing.
   b. Correct. Phishing involves email messages that appear to come from legitimate business or government sources.
   c. Incorrect. A rod and reel are used for fishing, not phishing. Email is usually used for phishing.
   d. Incorrect. A botnet is used for a denial of service attack, not for phishing.

2.
   a. Incorrect. A rootkit attacks the operating system, not an application system.
   b. Incorrect. A backdoor allows unauthorized access to the system, not a specific application program.
   c. Incorrect. A Trojan horse is a stand-alone program and does not attack a specific application.
   d. Correct. A virus is a segment of computer code that attaches itself to a program, such as Microsoft Office, that is already loaded on the computer.

The AICPA publishes *CPA Letter Daily*, a free e-newsletter published each weekday. The newsletter, which covers the 10-12 most important stories in business, finance, and accounting, as well as AICPA information, was created to deliver news to CPAs and others who work with the accounting profession. Besides summarizing media articles, commentaries, and research results, the e-newsletter links to television broadcasts and videos and features reader polls. *CPA Letter Daily*'s editors scan hundreds of publications and websites, selecting the most relevant and important news so you don't have to. The newsletter arrives in your inbox early in the morning. To sign up, visit smartbrief.com/CPA.

Do you need high-quality technical assistance? The AICPA Auditing and Accounting Technical Hotline provides non-authoritative guidance on accounting, auditing, attestation, and compilation and review standards. The hotline can be reached at 877.242.7212.

# Learn More

## Continuing Professional Education

Thank you for selecting the American Institute of Certified Public Accountants as your continuing professional education provider. We have a diverse offering of CPE courses to help you expand your skillset and develop your competencies. Choose from hundreds of different titles spanning the major subject matter areas relevant to CPAs and CGMAs, including:

- Governmental and not-for-profit accounting, auditing, and updates
- Internal control and fraud
- Audits of employee benefit plans and 401(k) plans
- Individual and corporate tax updates
- A vast array of courses in other areas of accounting and auditing, controllership, management, consulting, taxation, and more!

## Get your CPE when and where you want

- Self-study training options that includes on-demand, webcasts, and text formats with superior quality and a broad portfolio of topics, including bundled products like –
  - ➢ CPExpress® online learning for immediate access to hundreds of one- to four-credit hour online courses for just-in-time learning at a price that is right
  - ➢ Annual Webcast Pass offering live Q&A with experts and unlimited access to the scheduled lineup, all at an incredible discount.
- Staff training programs for audit, tax and preparation, compilation, and review
- Certificate programs offering comprehensive curriculums developed by practicing experts to build fundamental core competencies in specialized topics
- National conferences presented by recognized experts
- Affordable courses on-site at your organization – visit **aicpalearning.org/on-site** for more information.
- Seminars sponsored by your state society and led by top instructors. For a complete list, visit **aicpalearning.org/publicseminar**.

## Take control of your career development

The AICPA's Competency and Learning website at **https://competency.aicpa.org** brings together a variety of learning resources and a self-assessment tool, enabling tracking and reporting of progress toward learning goals.

## Visit **www.AICPAStore.com** to browse our CPE selections.

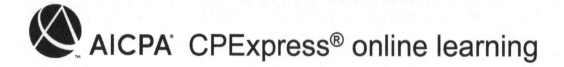 **AICPA** CPExpress® online learning

# Just-in-time learning at your fingertips 24/7

Where can you get <u>unlimited online access</u> to 600+ credit hours  (450+ CPE courses) for one low annual subscription fee?

**CPExpress® online learning**, the AICPA's comprehensive  bundle of online continuing professional  education courses for CPAs, offers you immediate access to hundreds of one- to four-credit hour courses. You can choose from a full spectrum of subject areas and knowledge levels to select the specific topic you need when you need it for just-in-time learning.
**Access hundreds of courses for one low annual subscription price!**

How can CPExpress® online learning help you?

- ✓ Start and finish most CPE courses in as little as 1 to 2 hours with 24/7 access so you can fit CPE into a busy schedule.

- ✓ Quickly brush up or get a brief overview on hundreds of topics when you need it.

- ✓ Create and customize your personal online course catalog for quick access with hot topics at your fingertips.

- ✓ Print CPE certificates on demand to document your training – never miss a CPE reporting deadline.

## Quantity Purchases for Firm or Corporate Accounts
If you have 5 or more employees who require training, the firm access option allows you to purchase multiple seats. Plus, you can designate an administrator who will be able to monitor the training progress of each staff member. To learn more about firm access and group pricing, visit aicpalearning.org/cpexpress or call 800.634.6780.

To subscribe, visit **www.AICPAStore.com/cpexpress**

# Your strategic learning partner

Let us help prepare your staff for the future.

What is your current approach to learning? One size does not fit all. Your organization is unique, and your approach to learning and competency should be, too. But where do you start? Choose a strategic partner to help you assess competencies and gaps, design a customized learning plan, and measure and maximize the ROI of your learning and development initiatives.

We offer a wide variety of learning programs for finance professionals at every stage of their career.

**AICPA Learning resources can help you:**
- Create a learning culture to attract and retain talent
- Enrich staff competency and stay current on changing regulations
- Sharpen your competitive edge
- Capitalize on emerging opportunities
- Meet your goals and positively impact your bottom line
- Address CPE/CPD compliance

**Flexible learning options include:**
- On-site training
- Conferences
- Webcasts
- Certificate programs
- Online self-study
- Publications

An investment in learning can directly impact your bottom line. Contact an AICPA learning consultant to begin your professional development planning.

Call: 800.634.6780, option 1
Email: AICPALearning@aicpa.org